NOSTALGIC LEEDS

The Golden Years

1900s to 1980s

First published in Great Britain by True North Books Limited

England HX3 6SN

01422 244555

www.truenorthbooks.com

The publishers would like to thank the following companies for their support in the production of this book

Main sponsor
Kingfisher

A. Taylor & Sons

Brandon Medical

Geo. Spence and Sons Ltd

Hall & Botterill Ltd

J & L Marshall

Jack Lunn

Joseph Geldart & Sons

Leeds & Yorkshire Housing Association

Leeds College of Building

Mone Bros

Redmayne-Bentley

Samuel Grant Packaging

Schneider Electric Ltd

T.F & J.H. Braime

The Donelec Group

Wilson Power Solutions

INTRODUCTION

This dynamic city means many different things to different people. The memories of living in Leeds or visiting the city for a special treat remain vivid. We were repeatedly told that these were the best days of our lives. We look back now and realise they were.

For a young lad whose only encounter with anything remotely exciting was watching the traffic lights change at Drighlington crossroads a trip to Leeds was something to savour.

The best time to enjoy Leeds - at least for a 10-year-old in the early 60s - was those quiet days between Christmas and going back to school in mid-January when nothing much seemed to happen. But with gift vouchers to spend at Lewis's in The Headrow, the promise of glittering shop windows still full of good things in the newly-opened Merrion Centre and tickets for the best seats for the Grand Theatre pantomime it was all aboard Dad's trusty Ford Anglia and down the A58 to Leeds 'the old way' - long before the M62 was even dreamed of..

First stop was Lewis's toy department where an early purchase was a green Vanwall Scalextric racing car – like the one driven by Graham Hill – to replace the car that burned itself out on Boxing Day. But the prize purchase was the Merit Magic Robot game which knew the answer to every question under the sun simply by spinning round in its mirrored box. What's more it was in the sale so there was still money left over.

There was no time for tea before curtain up for 'Humpty Dumpty' at The Grand. Stars of the show were Des O' Connor as Simple Simon and a Welsh comedian called Wyn Calvin who played 'Humpty'. I well remember the older members of the audience cheering loudly when a man wearing a red cloak sang about a desert. His name was John Hanson, most famous for his role as the "Red Shdow", the hero of the musical 'The Desert Song'. At the end of the pantomime we were all hungry and made our way back up Merrion Street to a fish and chip shop called Nash's. It's very famous and has been making fish and chips for 80 years.

Full of good food, tired but happy we found Dad's car and settled down in the back seat for the journey home. We were fast asleep dreaming of our next day out in Leeds before we reached City Square.

Leeds has changed beyond recognition in the last 30 to 40 years. The skyline, once dominated by mill chimneys (and the Quarry Hill flats), is now a futuristic landscape with magnificent structures of steel and glass changing shape and form from every new vantage point.

In the pages that follow you will be transported back to the Leeds of old – to the 30s with the ever present threat of conflict, the austere 40s and the 'never had it so good' days of the late 50s.

Through hard times and happy days Leeds has survived and prospered. We have only to look at the city today to see the progress that has been made and the achievements realised.

As the photographs show, Leeds has a history to be proud of but, more importantly, an exciting future to look forward to . . .

TEXT	ANDREW MITCHELL, TONY LAX, BRENDAN O'NEILL AND STEPHEN FIRTH
PHOTOGRAPHS	BRENDAN O'NEILL
DESIGNER	CHRIS THORPE
BUSINESS DEVELOPMENT MANAGER	PETER PREST

CONTENTS

VICTORIAN & EDWARDIAN LEEDS

Leeds General Infirmary is situated in the heart of the city and has a history of saving lives that goes back 250 years. Nowadays one of the country's top teaching hospitals, it has a reputation for excellent work in brain injuries, heart and lung problems and other major trauma. There was no such thing as a helipad on the roof in this 1900 picture, but the establishment was at the forefront of modern medicine as we knew it in late Victorian times. Its roots can be traced to 1767 when an infirmary for 'the relief of the sick and hurt poor within this parish' was set up on Kirkgate. A small hospital was opened near City Square and the move to the grand building on Great George Street, designed by George Gilbert Scott, made in 1868.

Above: Leeds Corn Exchange is still with us, but as a retail centre housing many shops that cater for a variety of interests in fashion goods, jewellery, health and beauty, along with all sorts of specialist outlets. The building was designed by the Hull architect, Cuthbert Brodrick, a man also responsible for the layout of the Town Hall and Mechanics' Institute. The Exchange's foundation stone was laid in 1861 and the building opened for business three years later. Regarded as an architectural masterpiece, the Corn Exchange boasts a handsome dome based upon the style that can be seen on the Bourse in Paris. The photograph shows farmers and traders conducting their deals in cereals on the main floor. It was a major commercial centre in its heyday.

Right: A new century had not long dawned as locals went about their business on Commercial Street. It was a time of change, heralded by the passing of the old Queen and the crowning of her son, Edward VII, as the nation looked to the times ahead. Within a few years, there would be electrified transport as trams clanked up and down, motor cars would appear on the streets and, as if by magic, flying machines would appear in the sky. This street now belongs to the pedestrianised experience that is part of modern ground level shopping. Many of the buildings seen here are still with us, though with different façades.

Scenes from each of the first four decades of the last century are depicted in this quartet of photos that show how Boar Lane was changing as the century unfolded. The shot of Sutton's Mantle Warehouse, on the right looking west away from the Briggate junction in the early Edwardian image, depicts a building that dates from the 1860s when it was occupied by Pullan's Shawl and Mantle Warehouse. It

became Saxone Shoes in 1908. In recent times McDonald's has been on this corner, with Burger King next door. Holy Trinity Church, dating from the early 18th century, is just beyond. Over the way was the Trevelyan Temperance Hotel, built in the late 1860s and named for the leader of the Temperance Alliance at the time. It is now part of the Marriott chain.

The view east from the same corner, seen not long before the start of the First World War, looks down along Duncan Street to the Corn Exchange at the end. When the 1920s arrived, trams had gained roofs to their upper decks as we can see in the bottom left photo, something for which passengers were immensely grateful, but there were still horses and carts dotted about that linked us to pre-war days. However, by the start of the 1930s, motor cars had arrived, giving Boar Lane a much more modern look(bottom right). This major city thoroughfare has an illustrious history and has had its name spelled in a variety of ways, including Bore, Boore, Bowre and even Bur Lane. Most think that the name originated from the Norse word for 'farmstead', though some suggest it meant 'borough' rather than any connection with animals. Whatever the case, Boar Lane, in its various forms, names and derivations has been here since at least 1207.

Below: Most of the main part of Briggate is now pedestrianised, as the recommendations of the 1963 Buchanan Report highlighting problem areas in Leeds were taken on board. But, in the 1920s, both public and private transport passed either side of the central reservations that were home to tram stops and toilets. On the right, as we look towards the Headrow, we could see Walker and Hall, a Sheffield based business of silversmiths and cutlers. It had other outlets in a number of cities in the United Kingdom, as well as overseas in Melbourne, Adelaide and Capetown. The company was taken

over by British Silverware in 1963. Further down, the Victory Hotel was built as a private residence in 1800 before becoming a coaching inn. It was demolished just before the last war to make way for an extension to Woolworth's. Leeds centre was originally laid out under the direction of an early 13th century Lord of the Manor, Maurice Paynel. He determined that Briggate, the road to the bridge, was to form the spine of what was to become Yorkshire's premier city. The street became one of Leeds' busiest commercial centres, especially after the cloth market moved here in Stuart times.

Below: What an awesome responsibility this little lad had as he tended the horse and coal cart in the yard in Holbeck. But do not worry too much, as this was Arthur Long, son of Joe, the founder of the haulage company of J Long and Sons Ltd. The youngster knew his way around, having been born into the business. Trade was flourishing in the 1920s and developed so well that Joe was able to expand and move to Cross Gates, where he opened a garage on Marshall Street. In the background you can see the top dome of the Queen's Theatre, built in 1898.

Above: The people in this late Edwardian photograph taken on Cross Gates Station all look very smart and dapper. The staff proudly wore their uniforms and the ladies appeared very chic and elegant in their long skirts and freshly starched blouses. There was not a pair of jeans or set of trainers in sight. No-one was really sure how to spell the name of the station as it used to appear as both two words and a single one on railway signage, all at the same time. What we do know is that it opened in 1834 for the Leeds and Selby Railway Company and must be one of the longest serving stations in the land.

Right: This was street cleaning, Edwardian style in the time leading up to the Great War. Brushes and shovels were the only mechanical aids available, but it is the nature of the clothing worn by the women on view and their general demeanour that say more about life back then than a thousand words can. The dresses and shawls look so drab to our modern eyes, but perhaps they reflected the sort of downtrodden lot that fate had dealt these people. When some talk about 'the good old days', show them evidence such as this.

Right and below right: These trams date from the early days of this form of light rail transport, as we can tell from the design of the cars as well as the clothing worn by passengers and Corporation staff. The vehicle heading towards the camera was coming along Chapeltown Road, near the junction with Newton Road on the right as we look. The handsome building on the opposite corner with Sholebroke Avenue is still there today. In the posed photograph, tonight we can see what a draughty experience tram travel was for both driver and upper deck passenger in 1910. Throughout most of its lifetime the tramway service used a mixture of bus style and balloon trams, both in double-decker formation. The system of electricity collection from the overhead wiring was unusual in that it used pantographs rather than poles, doing away with the need to turn the pole round at each terminus.

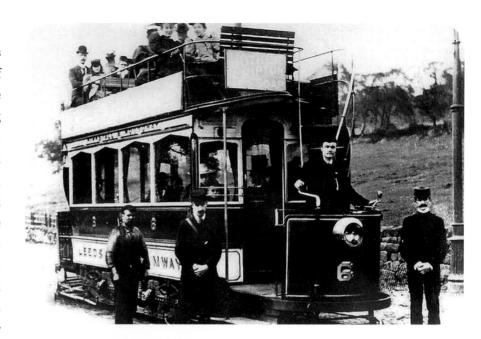

Left: Here we can see a photograph of Oxley Hall, which dates back to 1861, when it was known as Weetwood Villa, also called 'The Elms' by 1864. The fine building on Westwood Lane assumed its new name on becoming a residential hall for women students attending Leeds University. It was a gift from local banker James W Oxley in 1920 and included nearly 8 acres of land. The Hall opened in October 1921, becoming the fifth Hall of Residence for women. A new wing was added in 1928 after a brief closure and the hall re-opened with 65 students in residence. By the 1950s the number had risen to 138. The Oxley Hall was Grade II listed in September, 1969.

This trio shows us that our city is not all high rise offices and shopping malls. In fact, we have more green and open space than just about any other city of comparable note. So, let us be thankful for such idyllic havens of peace as Meanwood Beck. Here, 'in a shady nook by a babbling brook, mid the flowers', as Donald Peers sang back in the 1940s, we can enjoy the stream as it winds through Adel, Meanwood and Sheepscar before joining the River Aire. The beck was previously a source of water for the village of Headingley and two of its earliest bridges led straight to it. In the 19th century it supplied water for a chemical works and tanneries, one of which, Sugarwell Court, is now a university hall of residence.

The companion images are of Roundhay Park. Stepping into a boat on the Lower Lake in 1905 was quite a precarious job for ladies wearing such long skirts, as demanded by both fashion and standards of modesty. Also called Waterloo Lake, it owed that name to the soldiers who constructed it, having previously served their country during the Napoleonic Wars. The gardens and pathways provide lovely places where one can sit or promenade in tranquillity, just taking in the sights and sounds around. Those pictured in 1919 were glad of peaceful surroundings, having just gone through four years of hostilities.

CITY SQUARE OVER THE YEARS

Driving a laden horse and cart, such as the one in the foreground, would be risking death and destruction on what is today part of the inner city one way loop road. A century ago, this was still the centre of the Leeds, but somewhere that pedestrians and road users could negotiate much more easily. The Black Prince, astride his charger, had not long been in place back then. He took up his position in 1903, but his connection with our city is not just tenuous, but actually non-existent. The statue was erected merely because the figure represented someone of importance and the city fathers felt that the son of Edward III had sufficient historical significance to merit such a place. The sculpture was commissioned by local industrialist Colonel Thomas Walter Harding.

Above right: An unusual sight in Leeds City Square as a massive boiler or possibly a steam accumulator, is being transported across the city on the back of a Scammell lorry from Marston Road Services. Maybe the flatbed wagon is feeling the strain or the boiler has shifted, causing the driver to stop and check his heavyweight cargo. Certainly a small crowd has started to gather at the back of the vehicle to view the events. The load is on route from Leeds & Bradford Boiler Company, founded in 1876. At the time of this photograph in 1922, people were still recovering from the effects of war and this may have brought some light relief on a wet and windy day.

Below: The statue of the Black Prince was created by Thomas Brock, a sculptor who had come to prominence in 1872 when his Albert Memorial, a tribute to Queen Victoria's late husband, was unveiled. The Majestic Cinemas opened in 1922 with seating for 2,800 patrons. It was the premier movie house of its day and served the city well for the best part of half a century until closing its doors in 1969 and becoming a bingo hall. The first films shown here starred many of the greats of the silent era. Lillian Gish and Richard Barthelmess topped the bill on the opening night in in DW Griffith's 'Way Down East', while Rudolph Valentino, Douglas Fairbanks and 'The Vamp', Theda Bara, soon followed. Later it was turned into the Majestyk night club, but was gutted by fire in September 2014.

Above: Seen in c1928, City Square was a hive of industry, with people scurrying to and fro. However, the activity belied the general malaise that was affecting the lot of the working classes in those interwar years. This was the decade that brought us the General Strike in Britain and the Wall Street crash in America. The 'land fit for heroes' that Prime Minister David Lloyd George promised us at the end of the 1914-18 War seemed a long time coming. Wages were kept low and jobs were far from plentiful. The 1930s would bring more misery as the Depression years came along, with several million having no employment at all. Families went hungry as there was little in the way of welfare support in those days and future prospects were bleak. The statue in the right foreground was a memorial to those who fell in the Great War, as World War I was then known. It cost £5,000, a small price to pay to remember the thousands who made the ultimate sacrifice. The figure of Winged Victory hovered above Peace and War, in the forms of a female figure bearing an olive branch and that of St George slaying the Dragon. As traffic congestion increased, the memorial was moved to the Garden of Remembrance in 1937.

Above: The tramlines ran past the war memorial in this picture from the mid 1920s. Winged Victory, designed by HC Fehr, was dedicated in October 1922 and stood on her base of Portland stone here for some 15 years. She underwent several changes of address before ending up in Cottingley Crematorium in the late 1960s. The statue remained there until 1988 when the statue's condition was so bad that it had to be taken down permanently. The head is all that remains of the original and that is preserved in the City Museum. Over in the distance, the scene is dominated by the former Royal Exchange building.

Left: It was on 29 October 1891 that we became the first place in the country to introduce an overhead wire system to source the trams. They would be part of the scenery until a dank November day in 1959 saw the demise of the tramway. Powered in one form or another, we had had trams rattling along the carriageways since 1871. Several suggestions have been made in more recent times about reintroducing some form of light rail or supertram service, but the purse strings to enable this have remained pulled tight. This scene from c1930 shows the Queen's Hotel on the right and the Royal Exchange in the centre. The latter was demolished in the mid 1960s and today the site is occupied by the Park Plaza Hotel.

Double-decker trams and the early motorised vehicles, dominate this view on the corner of City Square, probably taken from the roof of Mill Hill Chapel opposite. This was the 1920s...famous for Flappers and fun, gangsters and glamorous movie stars...renown for the Charleston, the Shimmy and unending dance marathons. Radio and the silver screen were at the height of popularity, as the television had not yet been invented. On the left, is the General Post Office and on the opposite corner the Standard Life Assurance building, designed by Archibald Neill that was one of the most iconic buildings that Leeds possessed. It opened for business about the time that Queen Victoria passed on her regal mantle to Edward VII, but was demolished in the 1960s and rebuilt by Norwich Union in 1967. Infirmary Street runs to the left of here, with Park Row to the right. The site of the first hospital to open on the former road is now occupied by Yorkshire Bank. This is a rare snapshot of this very distinctive time.

Edward, the Black Prince, looks quite lonely as he surveys the panorama across the square. Work was under way in building the Queen's Hotel. This was to become one of the finest of its kind for miles around, just oozing Art Deco opulence and style. The original hotel, built in 1863, was remodelled with a Portland stone façade in the mid 1930s by architects WC Green and WH Hamlyn for the London Midland Scottish Railway and re-opened in 1937. The Queen's was the first British hotel to have en suite facilities in every bedroom. It also boasted double glazing, a fairly rare feature at the time, to limit noise pollution from the traffic in City Square.

Judging by the hoardings on the right of the photograph, alcohol advertising significant. Next to a message from the Co-op we can see a poster for 'King George IV' whisky. A slogan at the time was promoting the whisky as 'Outstanding in every characteristic of High Class "Scotch". Next along is alcohol advertising for Booth's Gin and Guinness.

Right: Looking to modern eyes like Dinky toy motors, the single decker buses vied for business alongside the city centre trams. We can see from this image just how heavily we relied on public transport in the first half of the last century. Car ownership did not become the norm for families until the swinging 60s and beyond. In the background we can see the Royal Exchange building, designed by Mallinson & Healey of Bradford and built between 1872 and 1875. The clock between the Daily Mail sign, was installed by Wm Potts & Sons Leeds in 1877. It was said that the Black Prince was pointing at a statue of Christopher Columbus positioned on this building, which was sadly demolished in 1966.

Above: By 1960 the balustrades and grounds in front of the old Post Office building had changed to take on a more rectangular, uniform appearance that would become typical of architecture and design during that era. The Post Office was built by Sir Henry Tanner in 1896 on the site of an old cloth hall. The intricately designed clock tower and the decorative chimney extensions stand above a building that also doubled as a telephone exchange. The collection of statues and sculptures depicting loosely dressed women supporting lamps was added in 1899. Over to the right, the Norwich Union building was erected in 1901 for Standard Life Assurance. In 1995 the cylindrical office block known as 1 City Square appeared on this site.

It was now a year after VE Day, but there was still a poster advertising the Women's Land Army stuck on the base of the statue of the Black Prince. This admirable organisation would not be officially wound up until 1949. It began life in 1915 during the First World War when women were needed to take over in the fields, barns and chicken runs from the farm labourers who had headed off to the trenches in France and Belgium. World War II saw the Land Girls back in action, initially as volunteers but later as conscripts. Although this image was one of peacetime, not everything had returned to normal when the final all clear had been given. Many servicemen came home to discover that family life as they had left it could not be renewed. Small children did not recognise their dads and 50,000 servicemen's marriages headed for the divorce courts.

You know the old story; stand around for ages and then they will all turn up at once. Well, this queue waiting patiently in the mist and damp would not have minded if just one tram appeared. All that was needed was transport home. Still, at least there were no bombs to avoid as Hitler and his thugs had been seen off the year before. Now all we had to do was rebuild our homes and factories that the Luftwaffe had destroyed. The markings on the pole are a reminder that hostilities had not long ended. The bands had been put there to help pedestrians and motorists find their way around during the blackout.

A SPORTING LIFE

Back in the days when plus fours were a commonplace form of attire on the golf course, a seed merchant and keen amateur golfer had the brainwave that a golf match between Great Britain and the USA might be an attractive proposition. Sam Ryder had already sponsored a number of local events, but it was the tournament that bridged the Atlantic for which he will always be remembered. An informal match between the two nations was held at Wentworth in 1926, but the first official contest for the Ryder Cup was held the following year at Worcester Country Club in Massachusetts. It captured the public imagination so well that the tournament was repeated every two years, with the countries taking it in turns to act as hosts. Moortown Golf Club is situated north of Leeds city centre at Alwoodley, just off the A61 to Harrogate. On a course designed by Alister Mackenzie, the opening drives were played down the first fairway in 1909. The club was given the honour of hosting the first Ryder Cup contest to be held in Britain when we greeted the side captained by the legendary Walter Hagen. Our boys were led by George Duncan (seen receiving the Cup from Sam Ryder) and his side included Percy Alliss, the father of Peter, a golfer who would also play Ryder Cup golf in the 1950s and later become an outstanding commentator on the sport. We beat the USA 7-5 in 1929, but subsequently struggled to give our opponents a strong challenge. To even things up, representation on 'our side' was extended to include players from mainland Europe in 1979.

These 2 photos of the successful Leeds United Teams taken in 1964 and 1968, were not only separated by just 4 years, but also by England's greatest footballing success, in the world cup of 1966. It is very much a case of 'spot the difference' between the images and there are a few, aside of Don Revie of course. The links with Manchester United were strong both in football rivalry and player transfers which included John Giles and Freddie Goodwin from 'Man United' and later Brian Greenhoff and Gordon Strachan. In the other direction went the likes of Eric Cantona and Denis Irwin whilst Gordon McQueen, Joe Jordan and Arthur Graham played for both clubs.

The later photo shows the successful side who won the League Cup in 1968 with the Division One Championship following the year after. Jackie Charlton towers above the rest of the team in both height and pride after the glorious English win in the World Cup of 1966 and stands along side his World Cup winning team mate, Norman Hunter

If your memory is good you may well be able to pick out: Back Row; Madeley, O'Grady, Harvey, Sprake, Charlton, Hunter. Middle Row; Johannsen, Belfitt, Jones, Hibbitt, Gray, Lorimer. Front Row; Reaney, Cooper, Giles, Bremner, Greenhoff, Bates.

In 1972 the team lifted the FA Cup after beating Arsenal 1-0 and Leeds United went on to great success in Europe. A magnificent team and one much loved by the people of Leeds.

Following such magnificent success, the manager and captain received awards in 1970, with Don Revie accepting the Bells Trophy for Manager of the Year whilst Billy Bremner picked up the Football Writers Association Player of the Year. Bremner went on to win 54 caps for Scotland. After the end of his playing career he tried his hand at managing Doncaster Rovers before returning to Leeds in the managers role, which unfortunately lasted only 3 years. Bremner was an ever popular player with his Leeds and Scotland fans and the 'fan mail' kept pouring in throughout his career. Sadly nine years after returning to manage Dooncaster Rovers again he died of a suspected heart attack just 2 days before his 55th birthday. A sad loss to the world of football and the people of Leeds.

It was 1966 and a great year for English football. Leeds United fans of all ages gathered excitedly to meet and greet their idols, Jack Charlton and Norman Hunter, with Les Cocker behind. Only a few days after winning the World Cup with England they met the Lord Mayor and Lady Mayoress at Leeds Civic Hall. Norman Hunter held a young admirer in his arms as she waved happily to the people around her. Both were enjoying an even greater degree of stardom than usual, following their participation in the wonderful success.

Right and Inset: There was always a euphoria which surrounded footballing successes and Leeds was no exception with 3000 fans turning out in 1964 to welcome home their heroes who had won the Division Two Championship. The team and backroom staff were arriving at the Civic Hall for the celebrations as this was not just important for football, but also for the city. Leeds was a proud city and with a football team entering the First Division it meant they would also have a crack at European Football. This would provide a real platform for Leeds business people to promote their services and products to a much wider audience. For the fans it would mean forgetting the trips to Leyton Orient, Scunthorpe and Luton Town and looking forward to visiting Old Trafford, Goodison and Highbury.

It was the diminutive five foot four inch, Bobby Collins who addressed the crowd and thanked them for a wonderful turnout. Don Revie bought Collins for £25000 in what seemed a risky purchase for a 31 year old at the time. But Collins repaid his faith in him, leading Leeds United to this Division Two Championship and later the next year leading Leeds into the FA Cup Final.

Below: These chaps looking through the window of the popular Granada TV Rental shop in Boar Lane Leeds in the mid 1960s were not watching the news or Coronation Street through the shop window. They were in fact glued to a number of Black and White TV's to watch the enthralling World Cup final between England and West Germany on July 30, 1966. England's victory over Germany drew in a record audience of more that 32 million, one of the most watched TV programme of all time. Colour TV did not become available on the BBC and ITV until 1969 just in time to see Neil Armstrong take his first steps on the moon, Concorde to make her maiden flight and the QE2 to set off on here maiden voyage.

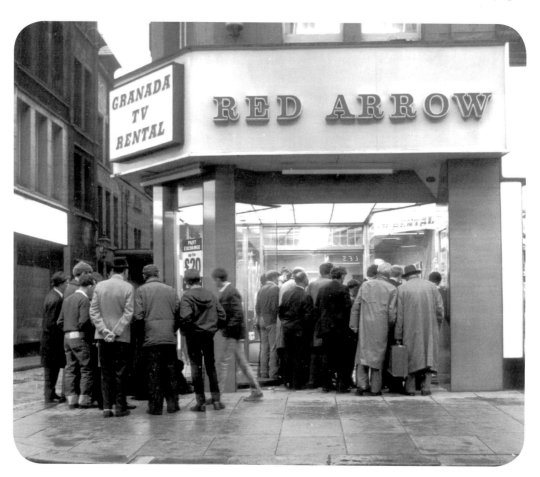

Above: Leeds also found sporting success with its dominant Rugby League team who played up at Headingley in this game against Warrington on 7 October, 1961. Eddie Waring , the great northern TV commentator would have loved the game and the 'up and unders' that this match gave. It was a rugged game which saw 34 penalties awarded but which left the final score at only 10-9 to Leeds, so some suspect goal kicking must have been witnessed. The try scorer seen here is the Leeds player Ratcliffe with the tackler Edwards unable to prevent the 3 points. The first rugby match played at Headingley was on 20 September, 1890 with the team Leeds St John's being a rugby union team, later converting to rugby league in 1897.

Right: It was not until the late 1950s, when the the 'Loiners' secured their first post-war Challenge Cup victory in May 1957, by beating Barrow by 9 points to 7. The young side being built began to show signs of what was to come by winning the 'final' in front of an 80,000 crowd at Wembley. In this photograph McLellan, the Leeds captain is being chaired by team mates after receiving the Cup from the Earl of Derby, Lord Lieutenant of Lancashire. Leeds tryscorers in the closely fought final were Pat Quinn, Delmos Hodgkinson and Don Robinson.

Leeds had not had a major sports ground until four local business men of the late 19th century came together to rectify the problem in 1888. They were WL Jackson MP, WB Nicholson (Builder), J Watmough (Painter) and CF Tetley (Brewer), who formed the Leeds Cricket, Football and Athletics Club with the first cricket game taking place in 1890. This team pictured in the 1960s was one of the most prolific Yorkshire sides of the era. With Brian Close as its captain it went on to win the County Championship five times in this decade alone. There were of course many other great Yorkshire players pictured at this time and included Ray Illingworth, Geoffrey Boycott and Freddie Trueman. Headingley became the home of Yorkshire Cricket in 1903 and continues to serve its county well.

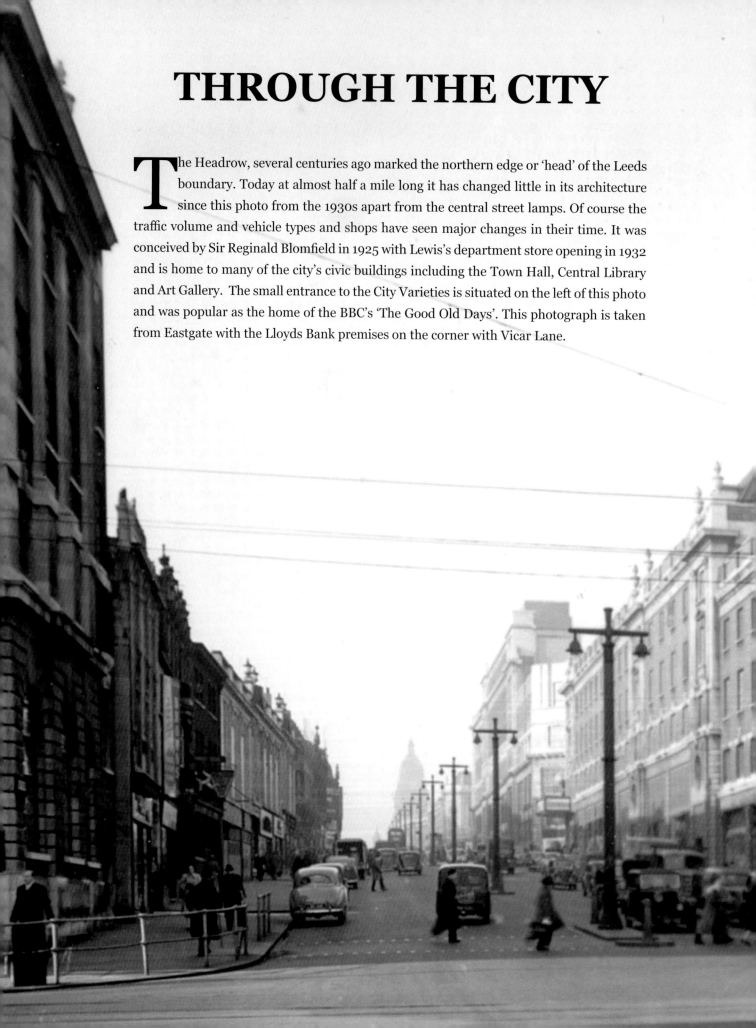

THROUGH THE CITY

The Headrow, several centuries ago marked the northern edge or 'head' of the Leeds boundary. Today at almost half a mile long it has changed little in its architecture since this photo from the 1930s apart from the central street lamps. Of course the traffic volume and vehicle types and shops have seen major changes in their time. It was conceived by Sir Reginald Blomfield in 1925 with Lewis's department store opening in 1932 and is home to many of the city's civic buildings including the Town Hall, Central Library and Art Gallery. The small entrance to the City Varieties is situated on the left of this photo and was popular as the home of the BBC's 'The Good Old Days'. This photograph is taken from Eastgate with the Lloyds Bank premises on the corner with Vicar Lane.

These various images from different vantage points show Boar Lane from the 1930s to the mid 1960s with the overhead cables for trams, appearing in many of them. The wide streets and junctions aided the movement of the many cars, wagons, buses and trams which moved goods and people throughout the city. The photo, in which the photographer must be standing in Duncan St, looks across the junction to the 'Fifty Shilling Tailor' shop with Saxone

Shoes on the opposite corner and was taken in 1943 at a time when most people's daily thoughts were still focused on the war. The white markings which can be seen on the pavement edges, were intended as a visual aid in these times of blackouts.

From the opposite direction we see a sunnier scene where the tram rattles its way towards us whilst delivery vehicles are parked to the left of this 1957 image. The next image looking back at the junction of Boar Lane and Briggate shows the large ornate building standing out, whilst prominently advertising Schweppes Table Waters in the 1955 photo. It shows a fairly relaxed city centre scene with the huge dome of the Corn Exchange in the background.

We see a more elevated shot of Saxone's, in the next photo, to see they have moved on to selling the ever popular Hush Puppies shoes in the 1960s with the C&A store further along having prime position on Boar Lane next to the smoke blackened steeple of the Holy Trinity Church. A vibrant and important area of the city, Boar Lane maintains its prominence in the city and no doubt will do for many years to come.

This is not quite a 'before and after shot' of the long established Firth, Ray & Prosser wallpaper shop in Wellington Street, but the fire in 1963 gutted the popular business premises as we can see from the view of the roof engulfed in flames. The fire brigade have several vehicles and tenders in place to try to stop the fire spreading to adjoining properties. In the distance, on looking crowds are kept back by the police cordon whilst the various services do their job. It was a devastating blow to a company established in Birmingham in 1871 but thankfully no one was hurt and the company continued to flourish.

The News Theatre situated alongside the grand Queens Hotel in Leeds had a very important role to play in 1953. On June 3rd it was the Coronation of Queen Elizabeth and we can see the large portraits of Queen Elizabeth and Prince Phillip sitting above the theatre entrance. The building opened as the News Theatre in August 1938 with an opening programme including, Popeye, Radio Parade and Golf Mistakes. However it changed its name to the 'Classic' in 1966 and then the 'Tatler Film Club' in 1969 but reverting back to the 'Classic' in 1979. It had specialised in providing a news service, including the memorable Pathe News for over 3 decades and although it only had 290 seats it was the place to catch-up on anything news worthy for the city folk of Leeds.

Here we see the cinema which opened on the corner of New Briggate and the Headrow as the Paramount in February 1932. The sparkling new picture palace delighted 1.2 million patrons over its first year alone. It was built for and operated by the American based Paramount Pictures Ltd. Taken over by Odeon Theatres in it was re-named Odeon in April 1940. At the time of thisphotograph in June 1947, the film showing was 'The late George Apley' featuring Peggy Cummings and Ronald Colman. Some years later, was even the site of three concerts by The Beatles (with Roy Orbison) in June 1963 and solo in November 1963 and October 1964. In an all too familiar story, the Odeon, which was the last picture palace in the city centre, was closed on 28 October, 2001. Today, the Grade II Listed building housing occupies the majority of the interior of the building on its upper floors, with a Primark clothing store in the ground floor space.

Below: Although Albion Street in Leeds has changed a great deal since the early 1960s, it remains a popular shopping area in the centre of this great city. It may be said that if the traffic volume seen in this photo had been the same today, the councils decision to pedestrianise the area may not have been taken, as only one car can be seen in the distance on the right. The timber fronted shops to the left, look like they are having the exterior painted and the shoppers are making a detour to avoid walking underneath the ladder. If the clock above the Boots store is correct it is almost two twenty on a sunny afternoon but with surprisingly few shoppers around. Could this be a Sunday at a time when trading on the Sabath was not allowed, with only the painter and decorator taking the opportunity of a quieter time?

Right: It's a bit of a wet day in Leeds in February 1955 and not many shoppers have therefore ventured out. A few cars still make their way up and down the Headrow and we might expect to see the likes of the Hillman Imp, Riley Elf, Humber Hawk and Vauxhall Victor, all engaging names for the then burgeoning British car industry. Looking along the side of Lewis's Store, which opened in Leeds in 1932 almost 76 years after Lewis's first store opened in Liverpool, we can just see the murky dome of the town hall in the distance. The time had not quite yet come for the now ubiquitous coffee shop where we would now pop into if the weather wasn't too good, so the option for the hardy shopper of 1955 would be to hop on a 'double decker' and head for home to sit in front of a nice hot coal fire and maybe have a well earned nap.

This photograph captures a view of the north side of Boar Lane in 1948. The tall and gracious, yet exceptionally grimy and sooty exterior of Holy Trinity Church dominates the picture. In contrast, on the right of the picture we can see the costumiers business, J. Jones. On the west side of the Trinity Church is the C&A department store. C&A had been here since the 1930s and many Leeds people joked that the letters 'C and A' stood for coats and 'ats. The initials are actually those of the company founders, Clemens and August Brenninkmeyer. We can just see a delivery waggon driving out from the roadway between C&A's and the church, not something we would see today, although the church does stand proudly as part of the very modern Trinity Centre, but having now been cleaned up for its new role.

Above: Today it is another pedestrianised area, but in 1956 it was still a busy thoroughfare for vehicles and shoppers alike. Lands Lane, just off the Headrow, provided an important connecting link in the centre of the city and clearly in this shot, the shoppers certainly outweigh the vehicles. The Yorkshire Evening news van has made its way through the traffic lights and crowds, whilst the two Rolls Royce's wait patiently for their turn to head for collection of their next group of dignitaries or theatre actors. It is a great photo to pick out the fashions of the time as well as the hard wearing coats and gaberdines which for some could literally last a life time.

Left: This photograph captures Cookridge Street on a cold day in 1956. Trams were still in motion on the streets of Leeds at this time, as you can see on the photograph. The closure of the Leeds system actually took place on 7 November, 1959. You can also see the incredible period motorcars parked casually by the side of the road. The introduction of 'Yellow Lines' in 1958 put a stop to all that on street parking! This was the age of cars such as the Consul, Zephyr and Ford Popular. By the end of the decade the famous and adored Mini was born.

Isn't it wonderful to see a much loved part of the city you grew up in to be retained and even improved for the pleasure of both Leeds people and the many visitors who so admire the city. The County Arcade is a prime and successful example of this, apart from the shop names and fronts, the arcade has kept its original splendour from the day it was opened at the turn of the last century. A great deal of work and effort has been put in to restore this great arcade with its ornate roofing and although the common place shop names of the 1960s, Manleys, Walcos, BSC, Phillips have now gone, major new stores have sprung up to ensure the County Arcade continues for hopefully another century at least.

Here are two lovely photos of Leeds Civic Hall in the 1960s, one an aerial view and one a little closer to the ground. They pick out both the architectural and community aspects of this fine building which was built at the time of the Great Depression in Britain. Ingeniously the council used government funds to support the unemployed by drawing up to ninety percent of its labour for the build, directly from the Unemployment Register. The building was opened in 1933 by King George V, who was accompanied by Queen Mary for the grand event. It was a challenging build as it was based on a sloping site, but when completed and clad with Portland Stone the building became an immediate success with the people of Leeds. This aerial shot, shows an already cleared car parking area behind the Civic Hall, but with long established shops and offices to the right, with the roadway running up to the top of the city.

As a lunch time picnic area for the workers and students of Leeds the Civic Hall gardens provided a pleasant sun trap amid the flower beds to have a sandwich and maybe think of things other than work or studies. A remarkable building and one of the best of its kind in Britain.

WHEN WE WERE YOUNG

Kids parties were always great fun and even more so when the whole street joined in and you could sit with your friends and school chums on a sunny day. These children and more so their parents would be able to breathe a huge sigh of relief as this party was for Victory In Europe day, May 1945. The residents of Park Street Leeds could welcome home their husbands, brothers and sons and forget the hardships of war including the blackouts and severe rationing of food and clothes. The gas lamp could be lit at nights and these children may sleep a little better in their beds particularly after the party food which may have been concocted from a little flower and granddads eggs, with a little sugar thrown in as treat. But what a lovely sight to see them all so happy after what must have been a devastating time.

Left: Not a teacher in sight as these young children sit happily on the wall of Brudenell School on Wellton Road, Hyde Park Leeds in 1949. The little lad standing seems to be keeping a few sweets to himself as he sneaks them out of his brown paper bag. Whilst the blonde girl in the foreground cuddles what must be her younger brother to keep him safe from falling off. We have to ask if this would be allowed today under our stringent health and safety rules, with playgrounds made of compressed rubber beneath the swings and at least one teaching assistant to every three children. It is a pleasant and unassuming photograph and can only leave us questioning the occasion. The old Victorian school was demolished in 1990 and is now replaced with a modern Primary School built in 1992.

Right: What great smiles on these chaps faces and why not when you could hold onto such a fine sledge and there was a good covering of snow on the ground. The wellies were always a problem, as cold legs became wet, the wellies filled with sprayed snow and sore red rings would become visible on the legs where the top of the boots would rub, but they were great for sliding and 'breaking'. It is of course a home made sledge and would certainly stand the test of time, with heavy wooden slats, a padded seat and strong metal runners. There were no plastic sledges in these post war days of 1951. The two lads are standing beside a local Leeds bedding manufacturers' delivery van which belonged to the family.

Above: This photograph was taken around the time of the 1953 Coronation, we can tell by the white commemorative mugs held by the children. The decorative pottery mug was given free to schoolchildren and made for the Coronation of Queen Elizabeth II. This is a formal day, the children are dressedsmartly – the boys with their knee-length socks and heavy-duty lace up shoes, the girls wear traditional knee-length dresses and Alice bands or bows in their hair. Most of them wear cheeky grins as they smile at the photograph. The young lad at the rear has a large fabric 'elastoplast' plaster on his right knee, no doubt from a previous accident so maybe his porcelain mug wouldn't quite last the day.

Right: The Women's Volunteer Service very much enjoyed their voluntary role, helping the old and young who were less able to fend for themselves. There were still many families in 1962 who could not afford Christmas presents for their children and the WVS stepped in to make sure that as many as possible were not disappointed when Santa was doing his rounds. This group in Leeds would collect, mend, package and distribute as many donated toys as possible to hospitals, children's homes and disadvantaged families. The dolls, drums and teddies were typical presents of the time and it would be many years before electronic games came on to the scene. In general the children receiving these gifts would be thrilled at receiving a patched doll or wobbly helter-skelter from Santa on Christmas Day, it would make it so special for all the family.

Right: Television had come to many households in the UK by 1963 and Leeds was no exception. This young chap had settled himself in to watch 'Andy Pandy' the children's favourite TV puppet show. He sat glued to the 'telly', albeit a little too close by today's standards, but the black and white pictures were a little 'grainy' and the broadcast scanning tended to leave horizontal lines rising through the screen. This looks like a 'coin slot' rental TV with the padlocked operating box on the side accepting half crowns and shillings, so lets hope the time didn't run out in the middle of 'Watch with Mother', before the episode finished "Time to go home, Andy is waving goodbye." A porcelain cat sits at the boys side and is maybe just there to keep him company, but we have to ask why does he appear to be wearing a gas mask box in the 1960s or has he just pinched his dad's Box Brownie camera for the afternoon?

Above: Boys would be boys and if there was any sort of a mechanical digger around it would have to be played on. But here we have a digger on a Bedford flat bed truck in 1960 and it was still a vantage point for these two boys. The haulage firm would have been taking the digger to site, although it looks a little precarious and would have been a tight squeeze, driving up the narrow tracks onto the flat bed. The lads don't seem to care however and were happy to pose for the photographer interested in capturing the scene for this Leeds firm who were prominent in the area.

Right: These Leeds children would have done what every other school kid of the time did and check to see which bottle had the most cream in it before picking it up and piercing the silver foil lid with the straw. As a food which could alleviate poor nutrition, free milk was introduced in 1946 with the Free Milk Act. The milk was stopped in secondary schools in 1968 by the Wilson government and later in 1971 by Margaret Thatcher ('the milk snatcher') withdrew this for children over seven. However many local authorities continued to provide free milk and in 1977 a European subsidy scheme was introduced which extended the provision of the service. This photograph is from 1965 and will bring back memories of morning breaks and the queues for these one third pint bottles, but they were a bit 'claggy' when too warm.

It was carnival day each year at the new housing estate in Leeds where the community was keen to establish strong connections between residents and organising a carnivals was one of the ways they chose. Each one had a Children's Fancy Dress parade, with prizes and a trophy which of course every parent wanted their child to win. The bobby in this 1948 photograph seemed to be holding back the crowds, although they didn't look to be too unruly. Amongst Indian Princesses, Little Bo Peep and a chef was the winning entry holding the cup, whose dress of 'sugar and spice' was her mothers theme as she sewed all those little sweets onto the dress.

In the later photo from 1951, the children sit together in their fancy dress on a warm summers day awaiting the judges decision. The little girl with the bandages and 'safety first' sign may well have been in the top three but those with turbans or baskets of food would have had the same hopes. Quarry Hill continued from its earlier beginnings in 1938 when its first residents moved into their flats. It was at the time the largest housing complex in the UK with modern features such as electric lighting, solid fuel ranges and intricate waste disposal system. Unfortunately some 40 years later following social problems and poor maintenance it was demolished in 1978. Many people outside of Leeds knew about the Quarry Hill flats as they were featured in the popular 1970s sit-com, Queenies Castle.

Above: With such a strong sporting pedigree, Leeds provided a great deal of inspiration for budding football and rugby enthusiasts. When you were kids, messing about in the mud was such fun and not to get into trouble for it was even better. The final of the rugby league school tournament we see here in 1972 had quite a unique talent in the shape of little Yvonne Davis, only seven years old but with at least equal determination as the boys around her. She is seen here passing what was quite a heavy leather, water sodden rugby ball, just as she is tackled by one of the boys from the opposition. Little Yvonne is clearly a match for the boys despite the ribbons in her hair.

Below: These two likely lads may well have been helping the local milkman on his rounds, all for just a ride on his electric powered milk float. They may have been there to guard the float in Moortown in 1975 from other children who saw the crates of milk as too tempting to pass by without dipping their hand into one, but they don't look quite big enough. Milkmen were part of the way of life in the 1970s and every housewife relied on them as the delivery of milk to supermarkets was still some way off and the local milkman would have delivered orange juice and eggs alongside their milk products. These types of pedestrian controlled electric milk floats were generally used on the shorter milk rounds which were not too far from the depot and later superseded by floats with four wheels and a drivers cab.

Right: It all looks a bit stark at Quarry Hill in the mid 1960s but a slide to play on after school was always a welcomed alternative to let off that surplus energy having been 'cooped-up' in school all day. They were never the safest of playground attractions as you had to climb the steps to the top which was a good 12 feet off the ground and then slide down the steel slide, hoping you didn't shoot straight off the bottom onto the concrete playground. With eight children on the steps and five on the slide these youngsters would need their wits about them to make sure they

didn't fall off. The more daring one's would have tried going down head first on their fronts or even their backs, but if things were getting out of hand no doubt someone from an upper balcony would have shouted down to keep them in order.

Left: Science fiction was a popular interest in the 1960s and robots were an important part of that. They were generally only thought of as TV mock-ups but Dennis Weston, from Leeds, proved the concept with his remote-controlled robot Tinker which was first shown to the world in 1977. The robot had 180 separate movements, 120 electric motors a TV camera and 29 channels for receiving signals from its inventor. Its tasks included washing a car, polishing furniture and even taking the baby for a walk, all viewed under the control of its inventor through a TV camera on the roof. We have to wonder what the baby was thinking and hope that he or she was not scarred for life by the experience of being taken for a walk by a large silver robot!

Kingfisher (Lubrication)
Greasing the wheels of industry

Not only keeping abreast of others, but striving to stay ahead of competitors in the keen markets of 21st century industry is no mean feat.

Over the years there have been troughs and peaks for Kingfisher (Lubrication), but this is par for the course in any market place.

Fortunately, this firm, founded in 1867 has seen more of the ups than the downs as it has ridden out the storms of periods of recession and uncertainty put in its way by the vagaries of global economics and local supply and demand.

Some of these outside factors are beyond its control but a consistency in manufacture and marketing, built upon a solid reputation, has helped to ensure the company's progress towards its position as a leader in its field.

Kingfisher's reputation in its branch of engineering has been established on a sturdy base with a strong business infrastructure that has been able to adjust to the changing demands of its

Left: A rare portrait of John Greevz Fisher taken around 1930.

industry, whilst still maintaining a solid reputation for products that are reliable.

This does not mean that Kingfisher rests on its laurels because it is always striving to seek out new and more innovative methods of manufacture that will fulfil client needs. In that way it can remain as a preferred supplier of high volume components to manufacturers reliant on grease fittings.

None of this comes without careful planning and an eye for the future, whilst always learning from the past. A programme of growth and development has been carefully managed, helping the company to establish itself as one of the world's largest and most influential in its particular niche of engineering. Kingfisher is rightly proud of the quality, service and technical support it offers in what can only be described as 'the complete package'.

Not surprisingly, keen attention to detail in the manufacturing process and consistency achieved in production are rewarded in the esteem in which the company is held by its customers who regularly see their expectations not only met, but exceeded. That is the main element of the reason why they return to Kingfisher

Below: The Kingfisher machine shop pictured in 1932. ***Below centre:*** *Raw materials stand alongside the finished product.*

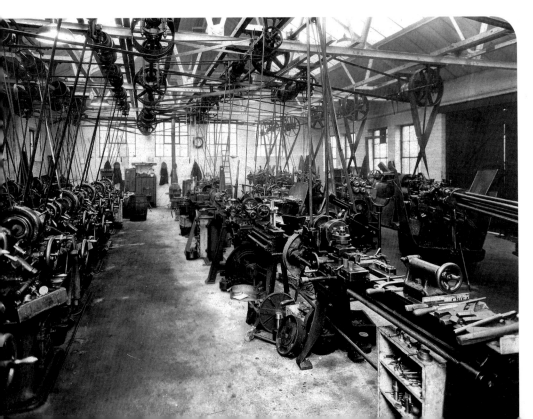

time and time again in the secure knowledge that they will never be disappointed.

To last for so long in the cut throat world of manufacture is a feat in itself, but to do so and retain a spot as a market leader takes some doing. For this, we must thank not only modern management and the skills of the present workforce, but also return in time to pay homage to those who laid the foundations and put Kingfisher on its feet as an infant entering the adult world of production and profit margins.

We need to go back about 150 years to start the story to an age when the Industrial Revolution

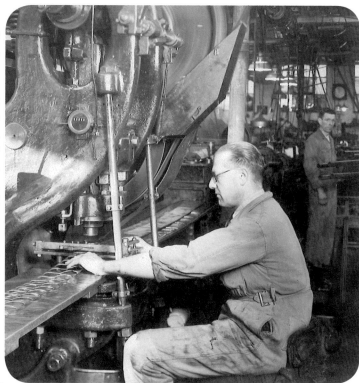

Left: Press operator Bob Shields pictured in 1944.

Henry Hillary Fisher was one of those who decided that life in the city was where his future lay. He set his sights on Leeds as place full of promise. It was already a thriving industrial centre in the north of England. Although largely the hub of co-ordination for the textiles, particularly wool and other textiles, its improving connections with major ports such as Hull, Manchester and Liverpool, as well as ease of communication with other parts of the country, made Leeds an attractive base. Technological advances and industrial expansion, allied to a central location in the country, made Leeds even more attractive to

had almost completed its task of turning England from a country heavily reliant on the land to one that had come to look to factories instead for its prosperity. People flocked from the countryside, abandoning the fields and ploughshares, to take up work in the towns and cities in the 'dark, Satanic mills' and their similar workplaces. Thanks largely to the growth of the railways, there was a much greater fluidity of movement than ever before. Instead of eking out an existence close to one's birthplace, people could now move far from home to gain employment or to set up new ventures.

a young man seeking his way in the world.

H H Fisher founded a business in 1867 as an oil merchant and importer at 3 St Columba Street. A sign bearing the name 'H H Fisher and Co' was still there on an archway leading into the yard, until demolition took place at the end of the last war. Back

Below: Kingfisher can claim to be largely self-sufficient, illustrated by the in-house manufacture of springs fitted as part of a grease nipple product courtesy of a single point coiling machine.

then, the street was a narrow one, crowded with warehouses and the like, connecting with Wade Lane and Woodhouse Lane. St Columba Street is now one of the lost thoroughfares of Leeds as it was incorporated into the Merrion Street shopping complex.

Back in 1867, Henry came over from the coastal town of Youghal in County Cork, aged just 23, but getting the business up and running was no easy task as he had serious competition, there being some 38 merchants operating similar companies at the time. But, he persevered in an industrial climate that saw men working a typical 60 hours per week that rewarded the most skilled men in engineering at a rate of the princely sum of sixpence (2.5p) per hour.

However, despite starting with little to call his own, H H Fisher made progress in establishing a reputation for quality and reliability. Within four years, he extended the lease on the yard he used to include the ground floor of the building within it. The cost of the annual rent was a mouthwatering £40 per annum; possibly equating to a five-figure sum in today's terms. It was obviously worth the outlay as it meant there was room now for expansion and a greater flexibility in the nature of the work undertaken.

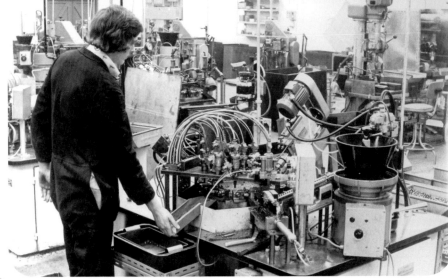

Above: Long-serving employee David Blackburn operating a new assembly machine in 1976. David, who has been with the company for more than 40 years, started as an assembly assistant and worked his way up to become assembly manager.

At first, it was all about manufacturing various greases and blending oils, but a start had to be made somewhere and it was by ensuring attention to detail and concentrating on a job well done that Henry was able to move ever onwards and upwards in his chosen field.

In 1875, Henry's cousin and brother-in-law, J Greevz Fisher, arrived from Ireland to seek his fortune. Life across the Irish Sea in Victorian times was harsh for ordinary folk. Successive potato crop failures in the middle years of the century, allied to continued impoverished living conditions, saw many driven to escape such a parlous existence. It was as an escape from poverty as much as a desire to seek fame and fortune abroad that brought Henry to England and it was much the same for J Greevz. There was little future for him at home and he was happy to throw in his lot with his cousin. The two men became partners and helped one another move the firm to even sounder footings.

The company moved from its original location in St Columba street, to an address off Sackville Street Ormonde Terrace, the building retained in the centre of the current site. The address was changed to Meanwood Road around 1967 but this did not involve another move. The firm took over the Royal Cinema site and converted it into offices spanning the corner of Meanwood Road and Sackville street with many of the "Ormondes" under its buildings.

Despite having had some success and with a seemingly promising future ahead, H H Fisher decided to emigrate to America where he would

Above and inset: Automation made a huge difference to output. Prior to automation this department produced 1,000 pieces an hour compared with 120,000 after the introduction of new processes.

spend the rest of his life. He died in 1933 and is buried in Norfolk, Virginia, as are his wife Edith, son and grandson, both called Arnold. J Greevz was left as the sole proprietor of the business and he became very much a Jack of all trades by dint of both ability and necessity. The demands were such that he was oil blender, accounts clerk and chief salesman, often all at the same time. With J Greevz at the helm, his energy and drive saw things move on by leaps and bounds. He had some 1,300 customers across the north of England on his books, all relying on his company to meet their textile and engineering requirements for greases and oils.

J Greevz Fisher was the driving force to end all driving forces. After several years in development, he put a new soap-based grease on the market. This product that he called 'Acme' was revolutionary in that it was the first of its type and boosted the order books and profits of the company substantially. Acme greases were not only able to withstand variable temperatures, but their use was appropriate to a wide range of industries that included not just textiles and engineering, but collieries, food processing, timber yards, railways and shipping enterprises as well. From the time he took over the reins until the First World War, there was a continuing demand for new grease products to meet the needs and changing demands of modern industry that would demand even more when hostilities began.

By then markets had been opened up across Europe and over the Atlantic. Because of Fisher's success, the new premises of Oatland Mills had been acquired in Ormonde Terrace in 1888. At about this time, the trade name 'Kingfisher' was set up and such lubricators as the Screw Plunger Automatic and Drop Sight-Feed components became market leaders. By then, a sales force of a dozen representatives had been set up and tinsmith's and a carpenter's shop were added, along with a brass foundry and extensions to the Oatland Mills site.

Either side of the Great War, J Greevz was joined in the company by his three sons, Don, Aubry and Persy. This promoted a change of emphasis in that more effort was directed towards the development and sales of Kingfisher lubricants and lubricators.

Right: *Adrian Fisher with the company's first female apprentice, Lynne Hayward.*

Above: *Chairman and managing director John Fisher inspects a large grease fitting a high pressure leak-proof valve unit used in tensioning caterpillar type tracks and one of the smallest grease nipples 1/4UNF straight hydraulic first invented in 1925.*

Progress was hindered during 1914-18, and difficulties continued post-war as the global economy entered a period of recession. However, Kingfisher survived and began to manufacture lubricators in a larger proportion in comparison with the greases and oils that had been its backbone in earlier times.

J Greevz Fisher died in 1931 and Aubry passed away soon afterwards. Control of the company passed to J Greevz's widow, Martha Marie, with the surviving sons as co-managers. Her daughter, Nady, would become a director in 1953. Martha's nephews, Adrian and Denys, the sons of Aubry and Don respectively, joined Kingfisher

just before the start of World War II and brought increased technical expertise to the company. Denys would find even wider renown in later life. In 1960 he left Kingfisher to found his own company, producing, among other products, the Spirograph, the toy of the year in 1967.

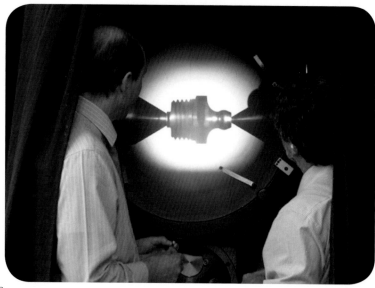

Left: *John Fisher and Richard Holt work with a shadowgraph which gives unerring accuracy through magnifying and measuring key components.*

Having survived the difficulties of the inter-war years, the company began to expand once more in peace time. New stores were built and workshops developed. In 1953, Kingfisher became a limited company under the chairmanship of Persy Fisher. A new range, Hydraulic Grease Nipples, was introduced and the success of this product, alongside its established BSSP lubricators, helped the firm to continue its rise in fortunes as the second half of the century unfolded. By the 1960s, a new and vigorous regime was in charge, buildings upgraded and new plant and machinery installed.

Things were on the up as a new period of growth was entered, helped by company stability as illustrated by having a third of its 68 workforce on the payroll for over 20 years. By now, Adrian Fisher had taken over as Chairman, a post he would hold into the 1990s.

Kingfisher (Lubrication) withstood the industrial unrest of the 1970s and the financial fluctuations of the 1980s to emerge still successful by the end of the century.

Below: *This aerial photograph, taken in 2007, shows the extent of the Kingfisher site. The business was established in Ormonde Terrace, Leeds in the area bounded by the three pitched roofs (centre). The factory has since extended to the right with the curved roofed building the latest addition.*

market. To do this it has developed a quality system that satisfies customers' compliance criteria for their continued accreditation to International Quality Standards. A successful audit from Lloyds has meant gaining ISO9001 - 2008 certification. A grease nipple might be an ordinary, simple item, but Kingfisher's dedication to quality high volume production of a low cost component provided the basis for success.

Wise investment on in-house designs, a determination to operate efficiently and a desire to involve a committed workforce in strategic planning augurs well for a concern that has already been ably served by four generations of a family that is still looking ahead.

By then the site on Meanwood Road, had been acquired and developed. Further adjoining property was purchased in 1997 and the company began another period of expansion. Despite this, the core business of grease fittings and allied products remain as Kingfisher's lifeblood. Even so, new ideas are always welcome and in 2004 stainless steel fittings were added to the range, with Monel, a cupro-nickel alloy also being used that has helped add business with the aerospace industry at home and in the USA. Additional business has included work for Land Rover, begun in 2010, when work on manufacturing a new roof rail bolt was started. Other developments include unexpected areas, such as archery. The present technical director, Richard Holt, is a keen archer and was very happy to see Kingfisher supplying a precision made weight for his bow that makes his aim all the steadier.

Now with John A. Fisher, Adrian's son, at the helm, this family business continues to meet the needs of a highly competitive and quality conscious world

Right: Technical director Richard Holt, a keen bowman, used his expertise to develop a part for a bow – a stabilising weight – that helps keep Richard and fellow enthusiasts on target.

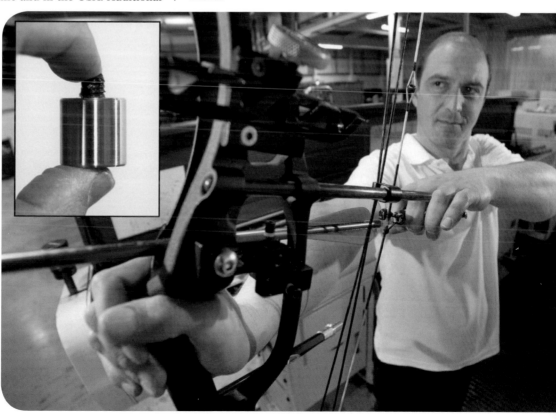

THE WAR YEARS

The red capret was was rolled out when Princess Elizabeth visited the WVS canteen at Leeds railway station. This wartime scene shows the future Queen receiving a plate full of specially made cupcakes, watched by a group of smiling servicemen. The WVS assumed the role of guides or information officers to the passing through troops. They had to meet the troop trains, day or night, throughout the war. The WVS also played a key role during the Blitz and offered comfort for civilians escaping from Luftwaffe bombing, in addition to providing support to firemen and ARP wardens, by supplying mobile canteens.

Above right: Curious crowds, gather round the wreckage of the Messerschmitt Bf 109E-1, in Leeds City Square, during the height of the Second World War. The plane didn't crash land in the city centre, it was in fact was shot down and crash landed in a wheat field at Mays Farm near Lewes in Sussex on 12 August, 1940. The pilot was reportedly captured and taken prisoner. These Luftwaffe wrecks went around the country as a moral boosting exercise, as much to galvanise support as anything else. Signs of war were very much in evidence in this image, with sandbags around the edge of the 'Square' and white markings on the lampposts and road kerbs, in the distance.

Left: Members of the Leeds Home Guard on a shooting exercise and target practice in 1942, using 303 rifles. Leeds own 'Dad's Army' defended railway lines, works depots and gas works. City Station, Wellington Bridge and the Canal Basin were guarded. From their HQ at Elland Road, around 15,000 men served in the 8th Battalion Leeds Home Guard with distinction during World War II. They stood down on December 3, 1944 with a parade down the Headrow. By comparison, the WVS (Women's Volunteer Services) had 10,000 members in Leeds.

We understand that during WW2, a bomber cost approximately £20,000 and a fighter plane £5,000. Leeds was amongst the first cities to contribute to these causes and to fund raise for the war effort. During 'War Weapons Week', 11 September, 1940, over £5 million was raised. We can see from these photographs that the running total was being charted on a big 'cashometer' in the City Square. This was assembled in front of the statue of the Black Prince and displayed the total raised so far. For every £20,000 raised another image of a bomber was put on the board. Despite the hardship and suffering the local folk of Leeds saved £72 million on war bonds, over the five years of WWII.

Left: Britain's well-known Prime Minister and the one of the most effective wartime leaders of all time, Winston Churchill, and his wife, the beautiful Clementine Hozier, take a visit to Leeds Civic Hall in 1942. They took visits to various cities throughout the war in an attempt to boost morale at such a difficult time. With five children, and Winston's chequered and varied career, eventually becoming one of the most influential Britons that had ever lived, Winston and Clementine had a remarkable life together.

Right: Under the banner of 'Lend to Defend the Right to be Free ', the military band was in full flow in Leeds City Square. The idea was to encourage the crowd to give more towards the war effort. The National Savings Movement was a British

mass savings movement that operated between 1916 and 1978 and was used to finance the deficit of government spending over tax revenues. The movement was particularly active during World War II in raising funds to support the war effort. A War Savings Campaign was set up by the War Office to support the war effort. Local savings weeks were held which were promoted with posters with titles such as "Save your way to Victory" and "War Savings are Warships".

Right: A delightful picture of two small tots shyly posing for the camera at the City of Leeds 'Spitfire Fund' event, launched in 1940. The official looking gentleman is dropping coins into one of a number of cradles set up to catch any hard earned spare coppers that might be thrown out of the large crowd gathered in Leeds city centre. It was a patriotic time and one writer hoped that his donation would be "another nail in Hitler's coffin". In the event nearly £30,000 was raised during the Spitfire promotion. The full cost building a Spitfire was probably between £8,000 – £12,000 (about £400,000 – £500,000 in today's money). The nice sunny day and the cute children gave no indication of the onslaught by the German Air Force (Luftwaffe), which began at the end of June, 1940. The Spitfires would make a massive contribution in the Battle of Britain and gain supremacy of the skies.

Above: Despite the inclement weather this group are dancing and jumping for joy, in front of Leeds Town Hall. This was a significant day in everyone's lives, as VJ Day signalled the official end to the war. Japan has surrendered to the Allies after almost six years of war. British Prime Minister Clement Atlee confirmed the news in a broadcast saying, "The last of our enemies is laid low". VJ Day was greeted with equal degrees of relief, euphoria and jubilation. Elsewhere in the city, thousands thronged in the streets to celebrate the end of hostilities and the dawn of a new era.

CITY OF LEEDS SPITFIRE FUND

CITY OF LEEDS SPITFIRE FUND

Here are two joyous photographs from 15 August, 1945, that give us a very slight indication of the joy and euphoria being experienced in the centre of Leeds on VJ Day. Outside the NAAFI Club, on Albion Street, there were scenes of jubilation and excitement at the news everyone was waiting to hear – the hostilities had officially ended, a few months after Victory in Europe. In the second photograph, a group that includes nurses, servicemen and cadets, may well have just come out of the NAAFI club, below, to join in the celebrations. We can see from the Leeds Industrial Co-operative clock on the wall in the centre, that it was just after 1.30pm.

In the main image, left, an excited group of uniformed merry-makers celebrate VJ Day on Albion Street by smiling for the camera. One lucky sailor is being kissed by two WAAFS. Similar scenes of joy were taking place around the country and went on into the small hours of the next morning, as people celebrated the outbreak of peace.

The NAAFI (Navy, Army, Air Force Institute) offered its greatest contribution during the Second World War. The Chairman & CEO during the war years was Sir Lancelot Royle and by April 1944, the NAAFI ran 7,000 canteens and had 96,000 personnel. The NAAFI clubs were available to all members of the armed forced and included a games room, small dance hall and what was most important to most of the troops, a canteen staffed by glamorous Naafi girls.

GETTING AROUND

By the end of the 1920s, horse-drawn vehicles had all but disappeared from city streets - the motor car was now king. Roads that had been designed for horse transport began to deteriorate under the steadily increasing load of traffic. The traditional 20mph speed limit was about to go, abolished in 1930 because it was universally flouted. This resulted in higher speeds on uneven roads, leading to more wear and tear on the vehicles. Fortunately local companies like Andrew Page had spotted the opportunity in what at that time was a relatively small accessories market, largely dealing with wealthy clients. Following a visit to America the business began importing some of the very first hydraulic jacks and lifts, and we can see an example in this photograph.

Right: Getting a baby and a pram plus a few bags of shopping on to a tram in the centre of Leeds, was no easy feat. The mother and baby in this photograph from 1954, are in a precarious position in the middle of the main road. There are a number of men standing around, but it is left to the tram conductor to give the lady the assistance she needs. The No11 tram is heading for the Gipton Estate a suburb of East Leeds. It was the first council estate built in 1935 as a "Garden suburb" for the working classes, with a mixture of 2 to 5 bedroom houses with gardens. Some 10-storey blocks of flats (Gipton Gates) were built by the council from 1956 onwards and 12-storey blocks (Briarsdale Croft) from 1963.

Right: Built by Brush to a Horsfield design, cars 187 and 155 stand side-by-side next to the interloper from London, the Leeds 501, former London Feltham 2099. After closure of the system, in 1959, the London Feltham returned to the Capital to stand in the Museum of British Transport, in Clapham. In the middle, the Horsfield car 155 was the first production car of this famous class of trams. Entering service during 1931, No 155 was built by Brush of Loughborough and gave 28

years of service to Leeds before the complete system was closed. Tram No 187, on the left, is operating in Crossgates (18) as a Middleton 12 Circular, continuing to Middleton and Belle Isle and then Halton via the city centre. After the closure of the Leeds system on 7 November, 1959, Sheffield became the last city in England operating trams, with Glasgow the last in the UK, closing in 1962.

In the early 1900s, vehicle manufacturers began building trucks for commercial use, or for shipping goods from business to customers. At that time, trucks were popular amongst business owners because of their speed and ability to carry large loads. Here in this photograph we can see one such haulage vehicle, carrying a settling tank for the Stanningley based Leeds and Bradford Boiler Company. This large cargo is to be delivered safely to ICI and the driver is checking the load is secure before he sets off. It seems fairly clear the journey would have been very uncomfortable and hazardous on solid rubber tyres. Scammell is, arguably, the greatest name in British commercial road transport, and their first lorry advertisement, used at the 1920 Motor Show, carried the headline "7½ tons at 3 ton Speed and Cost".

This is a sight you will not see every day as a convoy of traction engines pull a group of four 'steam accumulators', on an unmade road between Yorkshire and Lancashire. These light steam tractors, typically those weighing seven tons or less, were generally used for hauling small loads on public roads. Their unusual cargo are insulated steel pressure tanks, used to contain hot water and steam under pressure. They are a type of energy storage device which can be used to smooth out peaks and troughs in demand for steam. It's anyones guess how long the journey took, but 'at a snails pace', comes to mind.

Below and below right: Leeds City Station was completely rebuilt in 1967 when the nearby Leeds Central Station closed, and its services transferred to Leeds City Station. Bridges taking the railway over the Leeds and Liverpool canal were replaced, a new roof over the station was constructed and the newly created south concourse was the chief location

for shops, refreshment rooms and the ticket office. The City Railway Station became the main railway station serving the city. With 17 platforms, it is the second busiest in the UK outside of London. The original City Station was formed in 1939 when New and Wellington Stations were joined. Subsequent to the closure, Leeds Central Railway Station has been demolished.

Right: A less than happy scene greets this local policeman as he views the precariously balanced wreckage of the Leeds City to Scarborough passenger train in August 1961. The train came to rest on Lower Briggate Bridge, after colliding with a large diesel engine, just after it had left the station. The speeds of both the train and the engine were in the region of 10-15 m.p.h. The engine was not derailed but the leading two coaches of the passenger train were forced across the Up line and turned over on to the parapet of the bridge, which was demolished and fell into the street and the surrounding area below. Despite a rapid response from the relief services, unfortunately one of the passengers in that coach was killed and two were injured.

On 2 January, 1965, outside Quarry Hill flats, the latest strongman from Billy Smart's Circus shows off his strength. Unbelievably he was pulling a Leeds City Transport bus and passengers, with just the help of a rope, firm teeth and strong jaw muscles. A large part of the success of the circus was the showmanship that William 'Billy' Smart brought to the operation, the large family he could draw upon to run the shows and his ability as a showman to market and capture opportunities to advertise. Smart's Circus grew to be one of the largest in the world, touring every part of the British Isles. There was an excitement when the circus came to town. Local people would line the streets as the circus performers would parade through the streets by way of promoting the upcoming show.

Oops! and they say 13 is unlucky....not in this case. The No12 bus was involved in two seperate incidents within three weeks on the same bus route in Leeds. It was 18 January, 1966, when the jib of the crane crashed down on top of the double-decker. The bobbies on duty are trying to keep traffic moving along Briggate, outside Hepworth's Tailors, as the damage is being assessed. Fortunately, non of the passengers on their way to Vicar Lane were injured in the accident. The crane was being used to excavate a subway at the junction with Boar Lane.

In an unbelievable coincidence, the No12, this time on the way to Eastgate, was also struck by wayward steel, this time in the form of a girder. We can see it was 9.16am when the 45ft protruding steel girder came into contact with the upper deck of the bus, knocking out all the left hand side windows in the process. As the bus pulled in to the bus stop, suddenly passengers were covered in flying glass, but once again no one was injured. Bemused pedestrians and bus crew look up at the damage in Dewsbury Road, Hunslet.

This site, was first opened in 1938 and was known as Leeds Central bus station, although it is a good walk from the commercial and shopping districts, situated between the Quarry Hill and Leeds City Markets. The bus station was built at the same time and in the same style as the Quarry Hill flats, and we can see both together, bright as a new pin, in the image. Ominously it contained an air raid shelter, which could accommodate a mere 150 people. In later years, the bus station was used as the back-drop for the opening credits of Yorkshire Television sitcom, Queenie's Castle, starring Diana Dors.

This elevated photograph was taken shortly after the Lord Mayor of Leeds, Alderman E. J. Loy Wooter, unveiled a commemorative plaque, signifying the opening of a £66,000 major rebuild of the Leeds City bus station on 30 September, 1963. In the 1950s and 60s, use of public transport was a daily experience for most people, with a huge choice of routes, operators and vehicles to see and to ride on in Leeds. We can see by replacing the straight platforms with new ones of curved design full use has been made of the available area.

Above: This photograph takes a glorious journey back to the 1950s, when the coach was king. It had always been the people's form of transport, referred to by older readers as a 'charabanc'. Cheaper and more flexible than the train, it allowed those who had travelled little further than their own villages and towns a first heady taste of freedom. The distinctive livery of the different coach companies was part of a now lost world, when whole communities crammed into coach after coach en route to pleasure spots like Blackpool, Scarborough and Filey. With singsongs, toilet stops and the obligatory pub halt, it didn't matter how long it took to get there because the journey was all part of the adventure. In this photograph we can see a never ending line of Leeds based, Wallace Arnold coaches ready to depart to the coast on a Working Mens Club outing.

Right: People are walking past looking in the window of the Co-operative Society building in Albion Street but there was little, if anything, on display to see. It was March 1945 and still two months before the end of hostilities in Europe, which marked the end of the Second World War. Of the cars parked in front of the Co-op, the nearest is possibly a staff car and has a soldier in the driving seat, and a number printed on the door. It has only one headlamp; the car behind has a shuttered headlamp because of the blackouts. Some older readers may remember as a child, that the Co-op windows were a source of great amazement. They had concave glass, which meant there were no reflections from the street and gave the impression that there was no glass in the window. Times were hard and many will remember the Co-op 'Divi' which proved to be a life saver at times. 'Join the Co-operative Society - Save as you spend'.

Right: The landlady of the Ostler's Arms pub shares a drink with regulars under a copy of the Evening News from 2 May, 1962. We can see from the front page story that there was a threat of a 4d per gallon rise in petrol prices. At that time there were about 5 million private cars on Britain's roads – probably around 17% of the number quoted today. The tradition was that each days Evening News headline was displayed out of respect for the landlords journalistic clients, who were known to spend quite a lot of time there. Drinking was an essential aspect of those involved with the newspaper industry at that time.

Right: After the Second World War, Leeds set about building new residential districts or enlarging existing communities with new housing estates. This meant new ring roads and roundabouts along the main routes. This 1960s photograph shows the ring road at Horsforth, as one project was being completed. The stand out feature on the left is the Woodside public house, at the junction with Low Lane. During this period Horsforth grew and grew until it eventually became part of the City of Leeds metropolitan borough in 1974. Back in the latter part of the 19th century, it was considered to have the largest population of any village in the United Kingdom.

Below: In the immediate post war era, the Royal Voluntary Service, known as the Women's Voluntary Service, continued to operate as food rationing remained in place. Such was the work that it did, that the new Labour government funded the WVS from central government funds. In 1956, Queen Elizabeth II agreed to become patron of the WVS and ten years later, in 1966, she awarded the service the honour of adding 'Royal' to its title. This photograph was presumably taken just prior to that event, as the Royal (R) has not been added to the side of these Austin Cambridge vans borrowed from the Leeds Welfare Service. The organisation evolved to help isolated and lonely people, particularly the elderly. They are particularly well known as providers of the Meals on Wheels service which delivers hot meals to the housebound. In 1968, the Government dismantled the Civil Defence Corps, to which WRVS had been affiliated, and WRVS was registered as a charity.

Below: There is always a great deal of interest when a Classic Car comes along for sale at the car auctions. This was no exception when this beautiful vintage car probably from the 1950s, came up for sale at Central Motor Auctions in Rothwell. The immaculate car looks similar to an MG T-type convertible, and the new owner could now have been sitting on a substantial profit. Over 12,000 cars are sold through car auctions every week in the UK. Many of the world's most expensive cars have been sold at auction, a 1962 Ferrari 250 GTO Berlinetta is the most expensive car ever sold at £22,843,633, in 2014.

On 19 June, 1969 the 2,000,000th Mini rolled off the production line at Longbridge, the first British car to attain this mark. Sir Alec Issigonis, as he now was, was there with Austin Morris managing director George Turnbull. In the same month, a trio of Mini Cooper's would play a starring role alongside the likes of Michael Caine in the film 'The Italian Job'. The original is considered a British icon, an ecomony car built unabashedly with cost-cutting in mind. In this photograph is lucky lady, Mrs Swift of Leeds, who won a competition in the Daily Mirror to win the 2,000,000th mini. She received delivery of the car outside her terraced house in Leeds on 23 July, 1969.

Above: Captured over 60 years ago, the planes in this photograph are yet to get off the ground. The model in the foreground was a Chilton D.W.1A at Yeadon Airport on Whit Monday, 1955, during the second round of National Air Races, entered by J.E. Appleyard who was also the pilot. During the meeting there were a total of six class-races and 27 entrants. At the time, admission for adults was 2s 6d. Introduced in 1937, the Chilton was designed by A. R. Ward and Andrew Dalrymple, both graduates of the famous deHavilland Technical School. Their objective was to create a small, light sporting monoplane with good performance. The aircraft was of all wood construction, intended to be cheap to build and operate, yet have an exceptional performance on low power.

Right: A significant day in 1987, as a British Airways Concorde charter flight lands at Yeadon Airport. A year earlier, in August 1986, an Air France Concorde charter flight from Paris landed at Leeds Bradford for the first time, and an estimated 60,000 people were there to see it. Back in the day, Concorde was a supersonic passenger jet airliner, first flown in 1969. This turbojet-powered plane, entered service in 1976 and continued commercial flights for 27 years, until 2003. This event would have been an unbelievable futuristic dream for the owners of Yeadon Aerodrome when it opened in October 1931. By the mid 1970s the package holiday had become popular in the UK and in 1976 the first holiday charter flight to the Iberian Peninsula departed Leeds Bradford.

FAMOUS VISITORS

Right: Some readers will have enjoyed seeing Pingu, a playful penguin that has regularly appeared on our television screens since the 1990s in a popular animated series intended for young audiences. Actor David Hasselhoff was even persuaded to record a single called 'Pingu Dance', a portion of which was used as the programme theme song. Penguins have also featured strongly in the movies this century with such as 'March of the Penguins', 'Happy Feet' and 'Penguins of Madagascar' becoming box office successes. So, it is not a surprise to see that Kingsley, a King Penguin from a local zoo, had come along at Christmas time back in 1969 to cheer up the kiddies on the ward in Seacroft Hospital. He was accompanied by popular entertainer, Leslie Crowther, who had just finished an eight year run on 'Crackerjack', the BBC TV show that was screened on Fridays at 'five to five' and included the memorable 'Double or Drop' game. This image, though, came from Crowther's time on Yorkshire TV's 'A Merry Morning'.

Right: The great comedian Buster Keaton, star of many silent movies, came to the Leeds Empire on July 31, 1951. At Buster's request, this old fashioned selfie of him with George Robey was taken. It is believed at the time that they had never been caught on camera together before. The Hollywood legend was in Leeds and Bradford as part of a summer Tour of British Theatres in the 'Do You Remember Me?' tour. Renowned film critic Roger Ebert once wrote of Buster Keaton that he is "arguably the greatest actor-director in the history of the movies." His dead pan expression in all his sketches earned him the name 'The Great Stone Face'. Some of the stunts he performed were actually life threatening and unlike today, there were no high-tech harnesses or machinery to fall back on.

The Catholic Church of Our Lady of Good Counsel and St Joseph in Cragg Wood, Rawdon was, for most of the first half of the last century, a regular place of worship for the nuns who belonged to the order of the Sisters of Notre Dame. The small church, with room for a congregation of only about 120, was consecrated in 1909. On 28 April 1962, it was in the national spotlight when the actor and comedian, star of radio's 'Goon Show', Spike Milligan married Patricia Ridgeway. Milligan's first marriage ended in divorce in 1960, but his time with Paddy, as she was known, lasted until her untimely death from cancer in 1978.

It is hard to come to terms with the passing of time, but it is now over half a century since this quartet of Scousers crossed the Pennines and had girls screaming themselves hoarse in the stalls of the Odeon in November 1963. Surely that isn't Grannie tearing her hair out in ecstasy and Uncle Wayne waving his arms about with wild abandon? You know something, it could just be so. The Fab Four had topped the charts with their second No 1 hit 'She Loves You' and just released their follow-up song 'I Want to Hold Your Hand' that was destined to be another major hit, heading the rest of the vinyl 45s into the new year. It is strange now to think that the group had only burst onto the scene at the back end of the previous year and that their first tour in early 1963 was alongside such other acts as Danny Williams and Kenny Lynch supporting the headliner, Helen Shapiro. John, Paul, George and Ringo came back to the Odeon just under a year later and sampled some of the drinks in the hospitality area. By then, they had conquered America and the world echoed to the 'yeah-yeah-yeah' sound. The boys had even tried their hands at film making and their first movie, 'A Hard Day's Night' had just been released that summer. It included in the cast list such comedy stalwarts as Wilfred Bramble, Norman Rossington and Deryck Guyler. No-one was surprised when the title song went to No 1, just like so many others.

Right: The Beach Boys and Lulu share top billing at the Odeon, Leeds, in November 1964. A young looking Lulu, who was only 16 at the time, was happy to take a photocall with American rock band, the Beach Boys. The group's original line-up consisted of brothers Brian, Dennis, and Carl Wilson, their cousin Mike Love, and their friend Al Jardine. The Beach Boys' vocal harmonies are among the most unmistakable and enduring of the rock and roll era, with songs like "Fun, Fun, Fun", "I Get Around" and "Don't Worry Baby". Lulu was only fifteen when she hit the big time with Lulu & The Luvvers and their version of The Isley Brothers' "Shout", although she'd been singing in clubs in Glasgow since she was 12.

Above: He actually did not have much to laugh about on this occasion. Eric Morecambe, one half of Britain's favourite double act, had collapsed with a heart attack in November 1968 and his wife, Joan, visited him in the Brotherton wing of Leeds General Infirmary. Eric was only in his early 40s and the cardiac problem was something he could have done without, being at the height of his fame at the time. However, he and partner Ernie Wise returned to the limelight and continued to attract record audiences for their hilarious TV shows for another 16 years. Angela Rippon's legs, Shirley Bassey on a revolving stage, André Previn's piano concerto and Glenda Jackson as Cleopatra are part of British comedic folklore thanks to them. Eric collapsed and died just after finishing a stage show in Tewkesbury in 1984.

Below: Adam Faith (Terence "Terry" Nelhams-Wright) performs to the audience at the Chinchilla Club on Moortown Corner, in 1964. He went on to become one of the biggest pinups of British pop in the 1960s. First topping the charts in 1959 with "What Do You Want", which launched five years of chart success for him and made him one of the most charted acts of the 1960s. He finally gave up his singing career in 1967 and turned to acting. In the 1970s, Faith found renewed fame starring in the popular TV series "Budgie". It was the story of a self confident Cockney lad just out of prison.

In November 1961, the Duke of Edinburgh arrived at Leeds General Infirmary to preside at the ceremonial opening of the new Martin Wing and Link Block laboratory. Here he was accompanied by the Lord Mayor, Alderman Percival Woodward. The dapper consort of our Queen has always had a twinkle in his eye for the ladies and the nurses who greeted him were not disappointed. He turned to enjoy a cheery word with those who had waited to see him and they went home to tell all that the handsome Prince had taken time out to speak to them. It made their day.

'Coronation Street' was first aired by Granada TV in December 1960 when the Daily Mail columnist, Ken Irwin, gave it three weeks before the top brass of ITV pulled the programme. Little did he know! One of the cast on that very episode was Pat Phoenix, playing the buxom, chain smoking Elsie Tanner. The character she created was known as 'the siren of the street' and the scripts saw her falling for many men and being hurt by them all. As a sort of down at heel Diana Dors or femme fatale, she provided the sleazy sex appeal of the story line. So popular did Pat become that she was mobbed by adoring fans when re-opening the Shaftesbury cinema on York Road in October 1964, having had a brief life as a casino. She died in 1986, just after marrying actor Tony Booth, the father-in-law of future Prime Minister Tony Blair.

AT WORK

Nothing goes to waste in this nostalgic look back to workers at the Morley based Hailwood & Ackroyd shop floor. In the bottom left of the main picture, we can see the damaged lamps that had been returned for refurbishment. The company produced decorative and coloured glass products for industrial and business use as well as the home. In 1934 they would even manufacture Belisha Beacons, named after the then Minister of Transport, Leslie Hore-Belisha. The orange glass sphere was developed after much research work and put into production. Although they were made in Morley, surprisingly it is believed the local council refused to erect them in the city. We can see an early example in this photograph of an early exhibition stand, alongside a selection of classic petrol pump signs.

The manufacture of cloth has for centuries been an important occupation of Yorkshire men and women. There is proof of the existence of the industry from the 12th century onwards and generations of the people of Leeds have worked at the spinning wheel, the loom or the dye vat. The real boom period for Leeds was brought about by the growth of the great cloth mills in the nineteenth century. It was the Industrial Revolution and the introduction of machinery which made mass production possible and spurred on the growth of the mills. In this photograph we can see the all female workers hard at work, in the machine room at Dixon & Gaunt Ltd, East Street, Leeds.

Above: Although this was the 1960s, there was still a 'Make do and mend' attitude in the WVS (Women's Voluntary Service). There was still a sense of purpose and children's clothes to be made. Even in the days of free meals and subsidised school clothing, there were children in poverty who would be shivering at the prospect of winter and the prospect of chapped fingers. In order to help, the WVS members collected cast offs and material ends and turned them into sweaters and frocks. It was the wartime training that helped the WVS attach such a positive attitude to salvage and reclamation. In 1956, Queen Elizabeth II agreed to become patron of the WVS and ten years later, in 1966, she awarded the service the honour of adding 'Royal' to its title.

Right: The war changed the world of work for women for ever. When men went to fight, women were called upon to fill their jobs, and this included many jobs that were previously thought of unsuitable for women. In 1942 petrol rationing came into force and milk was delivered by float or hand cart, with women staffing each unit. Standard ration was 3 pints (1800ml) per week, occasionally dropping to 2 pints (1200ml). Pregnant women, nursing mothers and children under 5, had first choice of fruit, a daily pint of milk and a double supply of eggs. Here in this photograph, Mrs Ada Stone smiles for the camera whilst on her milk round on the streets of Leeds.

Leeds College of Building
Constructed on firm foundations

Over the years Leeds College of Building has educated and trained plumbers and plasterers, surveyors and site supervisors – all of them contributing to the changing landscape of Leeds city centre.

The provision of further education in construction in Leeds owes its origins to Leeds Mechanics' Institute which was founded in 1824. It later became the Leeds School of Science and in 1868 was transferred to the Leeds Institute building in Cookridge Street.

In 1908 Leeds College of Technology was established with its headquarters in the Leeds Institute of Building. The next 20 years saw great expansion and the college was organised under eight departments including building, electrical engineering and mechanical engineering.

The development of building courses in the late 1920s led to the need for additional accommodation and this was found, first at Roseville Road and then at Darley Street School.

In 1960 the Branch College of Building was established and just a few years later the college moved to custom-built premises. The name of the college changed to Leeds College of Building in 1970 and work on the new building was completed in 1972.

Above: The college's new state-of-the-art £17 million education and training facility – an 8,000 sq ft building which opened in May, 2015.

The college was extended in the early 80s and the number of courses continued to increase. Peter Shuker replaced Jack Place as principal, followed in 1986 by David Roberts.

To keep up with changes in the construction industry the college had to move into retraining but things picked up around the millennium and demand for construction courses reached an unprecedented high with waiting lists of over 3,000.

The college accommodation expanded, too, and a further five sites were opened. Ian Billyard was named new principal in 2002 and in 2006 the college was awarded a range of outstanding and good grades placing it in the top 10 per cent of colleges in the UK.

It remains the only specialist further and higher education construction college in the UK and has built an enviable reputation both regionally and nationally.

The college is often commended on the high quality tuition, facilities and resources it provides and this is reflected in the success rates of its students whose number has increased in recent years to around 7,500 due to the high level of interest in the construction industry.

Left: The opening ceremony for the North Street building which was completed and ready to accept its first intake of students in September, 1969.

A. Taylor & Son
Engineering through three centuries

It's been a memorable 12 months in the long history of Leeds based engineering company A. Taylor & Son.

Last year marked the 150th anniversary of the business, a celebration which coincided with one of the most significant events since it was established in 1864 – the relocation and commissioning of a new machining facility based at the former premises of H. Pontifex and Sons, a site dating back to 1796.

As the company galvanises its position as one of the country's leading sub-contract manufacturing engineers it can look back on how it has earned its reputation for producing 'Taylormade' goods – a sure sign of quality.

By the late 18th century Leeds had begun its dramatic transformation from a busy rural hub to an industrial powerhouse. The area's woollen industry led not only the West Riding but the world in textiles and Leeds went on to become a huge manufacturing centre for clothing.

However, there was a significant shift during the latter half of the 19th century after a devastating depression decimated the textile industry.

Leeds became known as the city where everything was made. Iron foundries, steelworks, brickworks and other industries employed thousands making rolling stock, cranes and boilers.

Above: *A large hopper fabrication, a bolted and welded construction.* ***Top:*** *A sketch of A. Taylor's original site at Weaver Street, Leeds.*

At the time it was at the forefront of the development of the steam locomotive – a coincidence that 150 years later A. Taylor's would secure the premises on Pepper Road where Mann's steam cart and wagon company built the first practical load carrying road vehicles.

A. Taylor & Son was established by Albert Taylor in 1864 during the second industrial revolution as tinsmiths and sheet metal workers in Kirkstall, Leeds.

Left: *Blue plaque showing historical importance of A.Taylor new site at Pontifex works.*

MANN'S PATENT STEAM CART & WAGON COMPANY LTD

Steam-powered road vehicles were built here. Previously Mann & Charlesworth Ltd of Dewsbury Road, the company produced unique designs of steam carts, rollers, wagons and tractors.

1899 - 1929

The business became general engineers to many of the aforementioned industries and during the war years its main product was bomb tail fins.

After the Second World War and the reorganisation of industry in Britain, Taylor's was highly successful as engineering resources throughout the country were in great demand. In 1947 T.W. Jeffery bought A. Taylor & Son from the grandson of Albert Taylor and this ended the Taylor family association with the business.

A year later Bill Benson joined the company and over the next 20 years helped expand the business by creating a large department manufacturing duct work for air treatment systems supplied and fitted on sites all over the UK.

As the fabrication division grew, typical products included steeping cisterns and grist cases for the Scottish whisky distilleries installed by the company's own erecting teams.

In 1957 Bill Benson was appointed a director and he continued to drive company growth, moving into bigger premises with

Above: Chairman Bill Benson (right) who sadly passed away in 2013.

heavier machinery to tackle much larger fabrications including hoppers, bunkers, chimneys elevators, conveyors and many other structures.

At the start of the 70s A. Taylor's began manufacturing small fabrications for the oil industry. This may not have seemed significant at the time but it would eventually prove crucially important for the future of the company and Bill could see this was a fantastic opportunity to move in a very different direction from the glut of other general fabrications.

After successful diversification and with the future in mind Bill set about negotiations to take control of the company and as T.W. Jeffery was looking to retire it presented the perfect opportunity.

In 1976 Bill, helped by his son, John, secured complete shareholding and now, in full control of Taylor's, they immediately started to develop the company further. The premises were purchased, additional overhead cranes were installed and the workforce bolstered.

Helped by these improvements and with a new focus the company secured multiple

Left: Prior to the oil and gas industry A. Taylor supplied fabrications to incinerator manufacturers.

Above: *Guidebase drilling template fabrication for the North Sea oil industry.*

contracts for North Sea rigs including guide base fabrications, 'Christmas tree' structures used on both surface and subsea wells, and drill templates.

Throughout the 80s and early 90s fabrications were becoming smaller and more closely toleranced meaning normal fabrication techniques alone would not meet the dimensional requirements introducing the need to machine parts.

Machining was becoming more prevalent and A. Taylor soon relied on a network of sub-contractors but during the deep recession of the early 90s many of these disappeared and for the company to continue growing it had no option but to venture into uncharted territory – machining!

In 1994 Taylor's installed its first machine tool – a Kearne Richards horizontal borer and almost overnight it became apparent that more machines would be required. Steadily, over the next 20 years

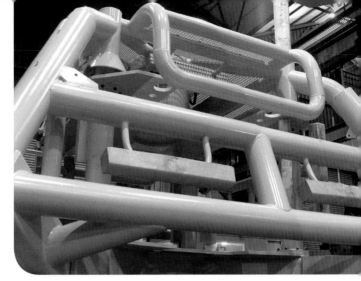

Above: *Overtrawlable protective structure assembly destined for Nigeria.*

the company purchased numerous additional machines making it one of the fastest growth areas of the company.

In 1995 A. Taylor & Son embarked on the largest phase of expansion at that time which was to build a 5,000 sq ft extension to its Weaver Street site. The new bay would house the much larger fabrications which the company was continuing to make and it was inevitable that heavier craneage would be needed to service the large manufacturing area.

Just 12 months later a 50-tonne crane was installed which propelled the company into a different league of fabrication culminating in the manufacture of the largest fabricated component in the company's long history – a 100-tonne continuous vacuum pan or sugar boiler comprising 3,000 expanded and welded heating tubes.

Below: *Purchased in 2010 A. Taylor take over the historic H Pontifex site in Hunslet, Leeds.*

Above: Turbine case fabrication machined at A.Taylor & Son.

By 2003 the investment in machine tools meant fabrication capacity was being compromised and after a long search a second site was identified and the company purchased its Modder Avenue factory, just two miles away from its head office.

Over the next six months A. Taylor relocated all its machine tools to this new purpose-built facility and also increased scope by purchasing additional plant to improve overall machining capability.

Another milestone was reached in2003 when employee Brian Smith retired after 50 years service. One of the company's longest-serving employees, Brian left school in 1953 at the age of 15 and started employment with Taylor's as an apprentice plater. In 1969 Brian was promoted to foreman, a role he held for the next 34 years.

Over the next few years the company improved its processes, increased its workforce and made significant investment in a bespoke 'material requirements planning' system to give effective planning of resources and allowing greater operational control.

In 2007 another long-established Leeds engineering company ceased trading and its site provided Taylor's with a perfect opportunity for further expansion. The site of Archer Engineering was based in the centre of Hunslet, an area historically renowned for engineering but more recently decimated as were many other industries in the Yorkshire region.

The Pepper Road site became home to the company's profile and material preparation division feeding its other manufacturing sites. The fitting and assembly bay which was housed in the machine shop at Modder Avenue was relocated to Pepper Road creating additional capacity which was much needed as clients looked to procure fully built assemblies.

Right: Spiral case fabrication for a hydraulic turbine installation.

Above: 3D Faroarm inspection used to dimensionally verify precision fabricated and machined parts.

Eventually all three sites were working at full capacity and with more machine tools sitting in storage due to a lack of floor space A. Taylor quietly planned its next phase of expansion.

Finding a suitable location large enough with both sufficient steel work and craneage proved difficult and after a three-year search the company considered building a brand new factory on a brownfield site.

However, fate lent a hand and in 2010 H. Pontifex and sons, a company established in 1796 making storage tanks and vessels decided to wind down its operations due to a downturn in business.

The Pontifex works were directly adjacent to Taylor's Pepper Road site so it made for a perfect fit and the two companies were soon negotiating a deal to ensure the tradition of engineering continued at the site.

In November, 2010, Taylor's announced the purchase of the Pontifex works and set about planning the unenviable task of relocating its machine shop to the new site.

The first project at Pontifex was to build a 9,000 sq ft extension which would house the company's largest machine tools including a recently purchased floor borer. The old buildings were gutted and over the next three years Taylor's created a modern well-appointed facility to house what was now an impressive array of machine tools, unrivalled in the current sub-contract sector.

The year proved to be a busy one. The company achieved accreditation to the new and very stringent welding standard BS EN ISO 3834 at the first time of asking. This put Taylor's in a very select group of welding engineers who had achieved certification.

Three years later the company applied to certify its other fabrication site Pepper Road and again this was successful.

To support the new site the decision was made to move the company's head office to Pontifex and further land and offices were purchased in 2012 opposite the works. With Pontifex fully operational staff finally relocated in January, 2013.

Above: Construction work on A.Taylor new site opened in 2013, Pontifex works in Hunslet, home to the companies ever expanding machining facility.

As the company approached its most important year in its long history Chairman Bill Benson sadly passed away after a short illness. Bill's vision over a 65-year period had seen the company grow from humble beginnings to stand today as one of the country's leading sub-contract fabrication and machining engineers.

Over the years throughout the success and growth of the company, Bill steered Taylor's through some difficult times but his ethos of honesty and integrity ensured customers would return and relationships would flourish. It is a testament to Bill that the company today works for three of the largest oil field equipment suppliers and has done so for over four decades.

Also celebrating a 150th anniversary in 2014 was the Leeds Rugby Foundation, a registered charity working in the Leeds community harnessing the power of sport to make a positive impact on people's lives.

A. Taylor sponsored a number of the foundation's events during the anniversary year and this partnership proved so successful the company continues to support them today.

Left: Funnel fabrications - typical parts that showcase the entire scope of A.Taylor services, fabrication, machining NDT and painting.

Above: Celebrating 150 years in 2014, a joint year long celebration with Leeds Rugby Foundation who were also celebrating 150 years of Rugby in the city. *Below:* A.Taylor opened training academy in 2013 and in the same year Gareth Longbottom won apprentice of year throughout the whole of Yorkshire.

2014 was an important year for three long-serving employees, purchasing expeditor Tim Edgley, plater at Weaver Street Les Foster, and QA engineer Alan Griffiths, all of them marking 25 years service with the company.

A.Taylor and Son prides itself on the high quality products it supplies and relishes meeting the challenges and expectations demanded by its customers in an ever-changing industry.

A firm continual improvement ethos means the company doesn't stand still, developing relationships with both customers and suppliers to ensure all stakeholders grow as business opportunities increase.

A. Taylor believes its future is in the hands of its employees, a highly skilled workforce which will not only maintain but also raise the standard set by previous incumbents. The company's training academy trains tomorrow's young engineers and already boasts award-winning apprentices who are leading the way in industry.

Further growth and expansion is planned as the company's core customers look to divest certain operations or outsource greater scope. In preparation Taylor's has retained capacity and future proofed its new site at Pontifex House.

By increasing scope and delivering a first class service the company is ideally positioned to take advantage and add further value therefore galvanising its position as a strategic partner to all its clients.

Hall & Botterill Ltd
Casting their net wider

Hall & Botterill was established in 1946 as an independent family-run cast aluminium foundry business. The company is an organisation with a skilled, dedicated and highly motivated workforce of only 11 employees.

The company has a tradition of product quality and delivery within 24 hours from receipt of an order from anywhere in the country. This is achieved by continuous investment and thorough updating the company's technology, capability and stock of products. Over one million castings are currently held.

The company is the largest producer of commercial vehicle corner castings in the UK, and the second largest manufacturer of cast aluminium rainwater products.

Hall & Botterill Ltd, based at Meanwood Road, Leeds, manufactures a comprehensive range of rainwater hopper heads and gutters, many of which are based on original Victorian and Edwardian designs.

Hand-made cast aluminium hoppers are manufactured to complement the company's cast, extruded and formed aluminium rainwater systems to suit round, square and rectangular down pipes.

The range extends from small simple designs to large heavy-duty ornamental hoppers. Decorative motifs, dates and emblems can be incorporated on many of the designs. The range of rainwater hopper heads can be supplied in natural aluminium finish or polyester powder coated in a range of colours.

Reproduction and new designs can be made to order according to customer requirements.

In its ornamental work, the traditions of the firm are steadfastly maintained, the greatest of care being taken in the making of patterns to ensure that its castings are sharp, clean, and full of character.

The company was established the year after the end of the Second World War by Eric Botterill and Leonard Hall and remains an independent family-owned business.

Both Eric and Leonard had worked at West Yorkshire Foundries on Sayner Lane in Leeds during the war. Eric Botterill was one of the foremost experts in aluminium casting. During the war Rolls Royce was experiencing immense difficulties in casting the Spitfire carburettor and it was Eric Botterill who solved the problem and eliminated the hold-up in the production of Spitfire fighter planes.

Leonard had gained a reputation as an exceptionally gifted moulder. He is fondly remembered by an apprentice in the late 60s, Erel Brown, who is now die shop manager. Apparently he could tell you everything you needed to know about a piece of metal by just looking at it!

The company began its life with just three employees from premises in Great George Street before moving to Meanwood Road in 1953.

Left: Co-founder Eric Botterill (left) at work.

Above: 'Big Betsy' was the largest gravity die cast in the world in the 1960s. *Right:* All available hands at work on 'Betsy'.

Using his vast experience, Eric built a foundry employing more than 60 men making power station components for Reyrolle, switchgear components for Ferranti, printing components for Vickers and Crabtrees, and Jacquard loom beams for Crabtrees. The company became, and still is, the largest manufacturer of commercial body corner castings. The largest aluminium die casting in the world was cast at Hall & Botterill's, at the time known in the foundry as 'Big Betsy' which was for use in power stations.

Eric was both Chairman and Managing Director of the firm from its inception in September, 1946, until his retirement in April, 1987 when his daughter Barbra became Chairman and Alastair 'Alex' Paterson was appointed Managing Director.

Alex faced no easy task. In the 1980s the general collapse of the United Kingdom's engineering base was taking its toll on the company. Alex's job was to turn around what was then a fairly bleak outlook.

The fact that the company operated from an old run-down mill meant that complying with an avalanche of health and safety, employment and building regulations issuing from both Government and from Brussels sapped time, energy and money during a very difficult restructuring process.

Until 1989 the company's main production was sand casting with only a little gravity die-casting. In a complete about turn the company now abandoned sand casting altogether and switched exclusively to gravity die-casting.

One story in particular illustrates perfectly the company's technical flair, its will to succeed where others struggle and its independent outlook.

Another company had been working for 18 months with an unlimited budget trying to make some castings for petrol tankers. but was having to scrap nine out of ten of its castings because of 'porosity'.

Porosity of cast components – gas bubbles trapped inside them - can have a significant impact on the strength of aluminium castings and great care must be taken to minimise the entrapment of gas during casting.

A friend of the company's buyer suggested that he go and speak with Alex Paterson at Hall & Botterill who was said to 'know a bit about die casting'.

The buyer arrived at Meanwood Road leaving the offending gravity die on the back of his wagon. As luck would have it Alex walked in past the wagon and took a brief look at the die before going in to meet the buyer.

Left: Every day presents a new challenge but there was - and still is – pride in a difficult job well done.

The buyer explained his problem - that none of the experts in the several foundries he had visited could solve the porosity in the castings.

Alex told the buyer if would cost £600 and two weeks to solve the problem. The buyer blew up and asked how Alex could possibly make such a claim when he hadn't even unloaded the die to have a look at it.

Alex explained that just from looking at the die on the way in he had been able to tell which toolmaker had made it. Furthermore in his opinion all the other people who had been asked had looked at the casting and pouring problem with tunnel vision.

The buyer was doubtful but Alex suggested that he left the die with him and if he could not crack the problem he would not charge a penny for the work.

Above: Managing director Alex Paterson demonstrates the new electronic factory gate.

In fact it took only a week for the firm to make alterations to the die and the pouring method. On the buyer's return he was presented with four 'unfettled' castings, exactly as they had been removed from the dies, which were then cut open in front of him using a band saw. All the castings were porosity-free.

The stunned buyer asked when he could have 200. Alex Paterson simply told him he could take them away immediately.

A white-coated clipboard-carrying inspector who had accompanied the buyer now produced a document as thick as a telephone directory and demanded exact details of how the parts were cast and whether the firm met the internationally recognised quality management system standard ISO 9001.

Alex Paterson's response was simply to state that firstly he was happy to fix the die problem for £600 but that he would have to charge millions of pounds for the knowledge that went into that solution. What's more, the firm did not have ISO 9001 since it was not prepared to reduce its quality standards for anyone!

Hall & Botterill Ltd fully recognises and appreciates the responsibility of the unique position occupied by its castings in the trade and neither effort nor expense is spared in the perfecting of its designs in dies and patterns to ensure the production of only the best quality work.

By 2006 the company was setting a year- on-year record in output, with 15 foundrymen using more tonnes of aluminium than when the workforce was 65. Yet remarkably, due to increased technical efficiency, the amount of energy used per tonne in 2006 was only a twentieth of that needed in 1946.

Left: Just some of the range of attractive and functional products made by Hall & Botterill.

During 2007 the company started to introduce the use of time-sequenced automated dies using 'Air Brains'. This meant that it was easier to operate a die with one man using less energy and therefore reducing the risk of injury

Three years later the recession hit hard and overnight the company lost a third of its business, which is why in 2010 Hall & Botterill Ltd reshored from Hungary a major company's suite of dies, taken on at Hungarian prices.

However, through using time-sequenced automated dies and rigs it turned into a profitable job. At no time during the recession was any man laid off, put on short time or on notice. Alex kept his workforce busy on a variety of tasks as the last thing he wanted to do was see the men go.

As business picked up so did productivity which was very high for the UK – but Alex identified room for improvement and once again he investigated the possibility of robotic fettling.

After much investigation and exploring ideas with robot integrators, Alex almost gave up; the integrators did not understand the concept of a 'jobbing robot' - one that can perform multiple tasks. Also, fees of up to half a million pounds were being quoted which to a small company is not feasible.

Alex decided to design his own Robotic Cell and pull in the relevant trades to assist him. At this time he was also learning

Top and inset: The Die Shop and Fettling Shop.

AutoCAD and 3D drawing, which helped in the design of the cell. By June, 2013, the cell was more than just a drawing - it was about to become reality. On June 10th, 2013, Hall & Botterill Ltd greeted their very own robot. Work soon began building the cell, sourcing tooling which in itself was not easy, most having to come from abroad. By August the business was ready to start programming, having employed the use of a robot programmer

Research and development never did follow a smooth path and tools had to be modified or renewed and new contacts sought. Meanwhile the workforce thought it would never take off – 'It's a white elephant' they said.

However, research and development being what it is, by the end of the year the robot finally went into production. It now operates five days a week but as with any project it is virtually impossible to program anything in because it is always working. Robotic fettling just hasn't improved productivity and quality, it has removed a great deal of the risk involved in fettling such as less use of the band saw and a massive reduction in noise.

As already referred to, Alex was learning AutoCAD and 3D drawing which has led to not only many certificates from City & Guilds but also the ability to design components. To this end the company has installed a 3D printer which now enables the production of prototypes.

More automation follows on in the dies. The company employs PC controllers to operate the dies, which not only removes the risk of repetitive strain injury to the men, but greatly improves the quality of the castings.

However, automation brings its own problems - the men have less to do but produce more and there is a constant drive to seek out new work.

The last quarter of

Above: *The company's skilled craftsmen are known for their attention to detail.*

2015 saw the arrival of Robot 2 but installation will be next year as a new building is high on the priority list. This same quarter saw the installation of a CNC milling machine, taking Hall & Botterill further by offering the capability of machining as well as casting.

As well as advancing working practices and capabilities, the firm's HQ has had a facelift. The yard at the back of the building has been concreted, improving the area for delivery wagons and couriers, the front wall has been completely rebuilt and an electric gate fitted. An illuminated sign also adorns the building.

Below: *Products are carefully stored ready for packing and delivery.*

Left: *The one piece sheet conveyor drum after casting.*

Above: *Manufacturing methods must continually adapt and evolve. Robot technology is becoming a fundamental feature of the production process making the working environment safer, friendlier and more efficient without the fear of job losses.*
1) The robot is delivered and prepared for installation. 2)The acoustic cell under construction. 3) Supervising the fitting of the robot. 4) The window hatch is put into position. 5) Receiving the air supply.

Any development needs soul and a sense of purpose, in Jack's book, such as these new homes from 2009 which are placed firmly at the heart of the community.

Jack Lunn

Building a living environment

The first thing that visitors to Progress House, Pudsey, the former headquarters of Jack Lunn, saw was an impressive sculpture placed in an alcove in the entrance area.

This piece of art work depicted Jack Lunn, the founder of the construction group that bears his name. It acted as a continuing reminder of the debt that the company owes to a man who was its founder and original driving force.

Since its inception as a small construction firm in 1949, what is now the Jack Lunn Group has grown into a multi-million pound business. Even so, it has kept true to its Yorkshire roots and focus, having had all its four different home premises over the years situated in Pudsey. It is, and always has been, a family concern with White Rose traditions of which it is immensely proud.

Today, the group can draw on nearly seven decades of experience and expertise that it can use to meet the demands levied on it by the requirements of office building, industrial and commercial, housing, schools, medical centres, private finance initiatives (PFI) and, not forgetting, extensive new builds and conversions within the Yorkshire Dales, in particular, Hawes.

Above: *Jack Lunn, the founder of a building empire and proud of his Yorkshire roots.*

However, it does not just erect structures, but also ensures that there is appropriate contact before building work begins by providing initial risk analysis, assistance with design features, co-operation on planning issues and the ability to offer a flexible form of work programming.

The company strives to ensure a proactive approach to any engineering demands and endeavours to be proactive in the way it tackles a job, while being adaptable to change. Over the time it has been trading, the Jack Lunn Group has developed a sound knowledge base that has helped it manage projects productively across a wide-ranging field, with values that can be as much as £12 million.

Some of these initiatives include partnered schemes, dealing with both private and public sectors, and can involve both listed buildings and new-build. Whatever the project, there is a desire to deliver quality on time and within budget and these aims have ensured that this company has become a watchword for good and reliable work within its sector of trading.

Jack Lunn was born in October, 1912, just a couple of years before the First World War began. Life was tough particularly so for those working down the pit. Jack's father, George, was a miner and this was no easy job in the early 20th century. However, George and his wife, Effaleine, created a happy family atmosphere for Jack and his younger sister, Dorothy - and that counted for a great deal.

At school Jack showed a special aptitude for joinery and it was this ability that helped him get a job as a designer and overseer in the shopfitting department of tailoring firm Montague Burton. Jack's role involved measuring up and producing technical drawings for

architects, joiners and builders who were to establish new retail outlets for the company. It was a very responsible position and Jack's expertise and know-how led to him taking on some night school teaching at the Leeds College of Art. He led classes in technical drawing and cabinet making, helping people not a great deal younger than him to develop their own skills.

Above: Jack Lunn's fledgling company had its head office situated underneath the arches in Stanningley.

By then, Jack had met his future wife at a dance at the Golden Acre Ballroom. He married Hilda Shaw in July, 1939, a partnership that would be a loving one for nearly 60 years. The following year, Jack went to work for Hilda's father, Henry, a partner in the building company of Cripwell and Shaw, based in Stanningley.

Jack was called up in 1942 and joined the Royal Engineers, taking part in the D-Day landings in Normandy and later serving in Holland. Having been demobbed, Jack returned to work with Cripwell and Shaw, but after the death of his father-in-law in 1947 he decided to start looking for a future under his own steam. He established an independent construction company in 1949 at Mount Pleasant in Pudsey and became something of an all-rounder by necessity, scouting for work, pricing jobs, purchasing materials and carrying out building projects as well as acting as accounts manager.

However, the economic climate was such that Britain needed to rebuild many houses, factories and the like after the ravages of the war and the work rolled in. Office staff were taken on and craftsmen employed and Jack Lunn Ltd was on the up. His friendly but purposeful nature, allied to a reputation for reliability, ensured that customers came back for more and new

Above: Roy Lunn, pictured with Rugby League personality Colin Cooper, is continuing the connection with Hunslet Parkside ARLFC. Jack Lunn was a keen supporter of the club throughout his life.

Above and inset: The 1960s property (small picture) is Cedar Gables, the house Jack built for his family. Styles and expectations change over the years and Lunn's have changed with them. They have been responsible for thousands of residential properties like this one built for Whitefield Homes Ltd.

However, it was, of course, tastefully and attractively done, with more than an eye for efficiency of layout.

Modern demands mean that everything grew to become bigger and bolder but the group still clings to those certain values that will never be outmoded. This means that there is still a focus on state-of-the-art as well accommodation that is purpose-built. The company has proved that these are not exclusive and can go hand in hand. When we moved into the 1960s, the country began to emerge from those darker days of the previous decade and started to celebrate the upturn in our economic fortunes.

ones were continually coming on to the books. By the late 1950s, the business was flourishing to a degree that demanded seeking out larger premises. The company had already moved from its first home to roomier workshops, but now was the time for even greater expansion. A former bakery garage, along with a large yard and office space, was purchased and named Progress House.

During the time underneath the arches in Stanningley, although work was coming in within the period known as 'the post-war austerity years', many of the jobs undertaken were modest affairs by today's standards. Perhaps that was a reflection of how Britons viewed things, living modestly within one's means. Even Jack Lunn's head office at the time was a comparatively simple affair, with an interior designed and fitted out by the man himself.

Right: Lunn team 1984: Three generations of the family on site in 1984, from left, Andrew Lunn, Graham Lunn, Roy Lunn, Tim Edlin, Maurice Reynard and Jack Lunn.

Above: *Some of the developments completed by Jack Lunn include houses in Bradford, Sheffield and Barnsley.*

Employment was high and wages had risen similarly. Families could afford bigger and better things and the purse strings were loosened. Banks were keen to lend to business and private enterprise was encouraged. New, affordable homes were demanded by newlyweds who had greater aspirations than their parents. An existence shared with them or consigned to a council house in a tired looking area was not on their agendas.

They wanted bright, attractive homes designed along clean lines, with garages, gardens and all the mod cons of life in a modern society. This was music to the ears of the construction industry and Jack Lunn and his workforce were happy to take on board these requirements. Residential properties on housing estates as well as those of a more individual nature were tackled with keen professionalism.

During this boom, Jack took time out to build a new family home for Hilda and himself. By then, they had three sons, Roy, Graham and Derek. Cedar Gables provided them with a house that was the epitome of the grand design of the times. It was so smart and up-to-date that it was featured in a copy of 'Ideal Home' magazine.

As time went by, the boys took on larger roles, though Jack would remain active in the company and continue as chairman right up to his death in 1998.

The company was restructured in 1980 and updated, with Jack Lunn and Company rebranded as Jack Lunn (Construction). The Progress House offices were refurbished, with Jack himself taking on much of the work on the detailed drawings of the scheme as well as overseeing the on-site progress. However, by this time his three sons were all on the board of directors and were playing their own significant parts.

Two different branches, Construction and Properties, came under the umbrella known as the Jack Lunn Group, but the one thing that has not changed is the pride in its Yorkshire heritage and the commitment made to developing the local area. That can be illustrated by such work as the housing developments on Otley Road in Bradford, where much needed affordable accommodation was provided, or the likes of the makeover to a leading boarding school in Harrogate. These are very different sorts of jobs, but ones carried out with the same intention of providing customer satisfaction in delivering an excellent service.

The company has a varied, high profile portfolio. It built a complex of 24 apartments on the former Kingsway Cinema site off Harrogate Road, Moortown and a social housing development in Chapel Alleron, Leeds, on the former Dominion Cinema site.

It was responsible for converting the Lounge Cinema, Headingley, for a private developer. It is now a complex of apartments with a convenience store at ground level. A complex of 48 flats was built at Neptune Street, Leeds, next to the river – all of this amply illustrating that Jack Lunn was one of the first builders to strart constructing apartments in the city.

The Group continues to offer support to less fortunate members of society, as shown by the work done for Leeds Council in creating Rainbow House, a new short breaks unit for young, disabled people and their families where they can enjoy superb facilities.

In 2013 Jack Lunn Ltd was formed. The company, run by Roy and Andrew Lunn, operates totally outside the Jack Lunn Group and is based in Pudsey where the Jack Lunn company roots originated.

Jack Lunn continues as a main contractor providing a construction service to a wealth of clients ensuring that the traditional qualities and values instilled by the founder, including the brand name, continue to prosper in the Yorkshire region. Since its formation the company has successfully completed housing projects for a

Above: *A sculpture of Jack Lunn is admired by his three sons, Roy, Derek and Graham.* **Left:** *Blooming lovely ... Jack's sponsored roundabout at Moortown.*

variety of registered social landlords in the Leeds, Bradford and Sheffield areas.

In 2015 the Jack Lunn Group of Companies (property, homes and developments) based at Progress House, Bradford Road, Pudsey, made the decision to move from its base to Harrogate. The group had operated from its Pudsey office since 1949 but after having been the subject of major changes within its group of companies the offices were too large and inefficient for their current activities.

Below: *Since the early days the Jack Lunn Group has embraced the concept of apprenticeship and actively supports Leeds College of Building. The company also holds its own 'Apprentice of the Year' events.*

Above: Angela Hudson, Jack's secretary and co-author of the Jack Lunn tribute, receives a long service award from Hilda Lunn.

This meant that by moving a new chapter for Progress House could be opened.

Roy and Derek Lunn have now retired but Graham is still with the group with special responsibility for leading the way in furthering the company's vision and strategy, with particular reference to regulatory and compliance matters. Roy's son, Andrew, is also a main board director director, ensuring that the Jack Lunn Group is still a family business.

Andrew has experience in a variety of sectors and has special responsibility for on-site contract management. But, it is not all building work and developments that make the company

Above: The young man taking his first steps on the career ladder is Derek Lunn, an apprentice in 1961. Rest assured, the company places a much firmer emphasis on health and safety these days!

such a success. There has to be a good 'product', but one that is delivered in a manner that is appropriate to modern expectations

This has always been important and no-one can fault the way in which excellent relationships with customers were forged in the second half of the last century and continue to be maintained in this one.

The Jack Lunn Group is well respected, not just for the quality of its work, but also for the manner in which it conducts itself. Members of the senior management team view having a hands-on approach as essential in building and keeping up the high regard with which the company is held, ensuring that clients feel as if they are getting true personal attention.

The founder set great store by high standards of workmanship and creativity, linked to consideration for both customers and employees. He would be well pleased with what he could see today.

Above: Jack Lunn's descendants, just like the founder, would always prefer the building site to the boardroom. Hands on is Andrew Lunn (right).

He dedicated 80 years of his life to the construction industry and his legacy continues today.

Samuel Grant Packaging
They've got it all wrapped up

The company newsletter tells you all you need to know about Samuel Grant Packaging.

Take issue no.3 for example. Of course, the headline news focuses on results – and what results they are.

Last year's performance was confirmed as the best ever with sales records tumbling in all branches. Leeds topped £12 million, the north east hit the £4 million mark, Sheffield £6 million and the furniture and play equipment arm of the business, Marmax, is about to break through £3 million.

With a certain amount of understatement, chairman and joint managing director Andrew Grant described the record-breaking year as 'very successful indeed'.

But that's only part of the story recorded in the newsletter, most of which illustrates the emphasis the company places on having a long-serving and committed staff.

The list of contents reveals new starters, long service awards, good news stories and claims to fame such as the efforts of the team in Sheffield which raised £110 for St Luke's Hospice by preparing lunch for their fellow employees.

The company matches all employees' endeavours pound for pound and, as a result, has given thousands to charity in the last year alone.

Top: Founder Samuel Grant. Left: The business relocated to Aire Street in 1898.

The business is a real family affair and there is no doubt among the people who have followed Samuel Grant that this is the open secret of the company's success. Samuel Grant would surely have approved of the company's ethos as it approaches its 125th anniversary.

He could have had little idea, though, just how the business would grow since he first set up The Samuel Grant Company in 1891, describing himself as a school furnisher. He set up premises in White Horse Street near to Leeds city centre and almost straight away had a stroke of fortune.

Samuel's former employer, the Northern Industrial Trading Company, closed down and he was able to snap up all its stock at a knockdown price.

Goods of all kinds were shipped into the city via Leeds-Liverpool canal and railways and delivered to Samuel's warehouse by horse-drawn vehicles.

Within just a few years the business was expanding steadily and Samuel decided to relocate to Aire Street in 1898 bringing it closer to railway stations, the canal and the developing road network.

Samuel recorded a major coup two years later when tailor Montague Burton approached him and asked if he could supply him with brown wrapping paper in which he could pack his suits.

Samuel could – and this was the start of a relationship that saw Grant's supplying paper products to Burton's for the best part of 90 years. He also provided Burton's with pattern paper - a premium quality rigid paper typically used in the bespoke tailoring sector.

The product became so popular that it was trademarked as 'Grancut' which continued to be a best-seller until the decline of the British textile industry in the latter years of the 20th century.

Another unexpected contract came Grant's way around 1900 - rhubarb wrappings! Yorkshire is famous for its rhubarb, most of which is cultivated in a triangle bound by Wakefield, Morley and Rothwell. From the first decade of the 20th century to 1939 the rhubarb industry expanded and at its peak covered an area of about 30 square miles.

West Yorkshire produced 90 per cent of the world's winter forced rhubarb - claimed to ease constipation - from the forcing sheds that were common across the fields there and it had to be wrapped in something suitable.

Enter Samuel Grant's which signed a lucrative deal to supply purple tissue paper - and millions of rubber bands – to wrap it for distribution.

By 1914 paper merchanting had overtaken the school furnishings side of the business and in 1921 Samuel Grant was incorporated and became known as Samuel Grant Ltd.

Samuel's son, Gordon, joined the business in 1923 taking charge of the packaging side of the business and he was followed four years later by Samuel's second son, Alan, who looked after educational supplies, providing school books and stationery.

Their father, the business's founder, died in 1939. By then he had sown the seeds of a diverse and hugely successful company with the potential to go on to even greater things.

Above: David Grant at the wheel with (from left) Matthew Grant, Sheelagh Grant and Andrew Grant in 2006.

In 1950 premises at Garnet Road, Leeds, were bought to allow for further expansion and a van and lorry were purchased to provide an even better service to customers.

Gordon set about extending the packaging range to include chipboard, boxboard, corrugated paper, waxed kraft papers and waterproof papers. Meanwhile, the educational supplies side of the business showed signs of shrinking in favour of other areas of the company.

In 1959 David Grant - Alan's son and Samuel's grandson - joined the business at the start of a career which saw him rise to the role of chairman.

Above: Garnet Road in 1988. Left: A delivery van in the 1950s.

It was not long before he spotted further opportunities for the business to diversify and he introduced cellulose tape to the UK adhesive tape market. In the mid-1960s polythene was introduced and David again was quick to seize the initiative for Grant's. In 1970 a new two-storey warehouse was commissioned to deal with the demand for polythene bags and building films for the construction industry. Not long afterwards, David purchased Thomas Lumb and Co, a small Yorkshire paper and packaging firm.

In 1973 Alan Grant died and the educational supplies arm of the business was reduced as a result.

An arson attack on a warehouse destroyed what remained of educational supplies and the decision was taken not to replace it. Instead, a new floor, the conversion floor, was built.

Meanwhile, David was investing substantial amounts into paper processing machinery, giving Grant's an unrivalled flexibility, speed and quality of service.

In 1978, Grant's bought Bradford-based CL Plastics Ltd enabling the company to take the next step into polythene manufacturing. Newer, sophisticated machines were brought in enabling the company to offer bespoke polymer recipes designed to customers' own specific requirements. Offices were extended further increasing the original 1950s accommodation six-fold.

A new 5,000 sq ft warehouse was added and Grant's was one of the first businesses to invest in the new Telex machines. The demise of educational supplies, or scholastics as it had become known, came in 1982, the last delivery of equipment going out to Bradford Grammar School.

Left: A warehouse fire in September, 1974 caused considerable damage. Above: A paper sheeting machine - an example of the investment in technology.

Above: Samuel Grant Ltd celebrating the company's centenary in 1991.

Samuel Grant Ltd, including CL Plastics, was now officially the largest paper, polythene and packaging merchant in the north of England. At virtually the same time, the order book of Harwell Packaging, a firm specialising in corrugated products, foam and void fill solutions such as bubble wrap, was bought.

In 1986 Gordon Grant died and David took over the chairmanship. His brother-in-law, Dr Ivan Ficenec, a Czech engineer, took up office space and had the ability to translate, enabling business with Eastern European mills.

Personalised adhesive tapes were introduced in the mid-80s and demand quickly outstripped supply. Huddersfield company Hawksmoor Tapes Ltd was bought and became a wholly owned subsidiary of Samuel Grant Ltd allowing the company to meet the increasing demand.

Hawksmoor, which had more than 5,000 print designs on file, relocated to Leeds. At the same

Right: Erik Dawid and Dougie Gordon Smith reading a Telex message in March, 1987.

time spark-free lighting and huge extraction fans were introduced to remove flammable fumes from solvents used in tape printing.

In 1988 CL Plastics successfully bid for a contract to create 'crop cover' – a revolutionary heavy gauge polythene designed to cover fields in Lincolnshire forcing carrots to reach maturity earlier.

Technology was moving at a rate of knots and Grant's operation - always ahead of its time ¬- was fully computerised in 1988. A fourth printer and laminating machine was bought to cope with additional Hawksmoor business and meet the need for laminated printed tapes for chemical labels.

Grant's celebrated its centenary in 1991 and marked the event by presenting staff with gifts and a tax-free bonus as well as hosting a dinner dance. In the same year Ladpack Supplies was taken over to form the new Samuel Grant (Sheffield).

More office space was needed and to address this Grant's bought the National Federation of Fish Friers headquarters. Around the same time the paper and packaging company Leete and Co (Cheshire) was purchased to form Samuel Grant (North West) Ltd.

In 1993 Andrew Grant, Samuel's great grandson and David's son, took over the running of the North West company, having shadowed his father in Leeds and working at CL Plastics to learn about the polythene side of the business. In the same year Jay Bee Plastiks, of Stanley, County Durham, was bought and became Samuel Grant (North East).

A significant purchase was completed with the acquisition of Marmax Products Ltd in 1998. Marmax is one of the market leaders in the manufacture of recycled plastic products, supplying a wide range of items including produce boxes, outdoor furniture and boardwalks to schools, councils and industry. Matthew Grant, David's younger son, took the helm of what is now Marmax Recycled Products having worked at the north east branch for a couple of years to learn the ropes. He landed a contract to produce plastic boxes for Morrisons Supermarkets to avoid issues with wood splintering. Box manufacturing moved to Leeds while furniture products remained in Caistor.

The order book for S. Milnes Packaging, Brighouse, was purchased and the company's first website went live. Marmax products relocated to Stanley where there was room for further expansion, the business developing into a highly successful company.

The order book of packaging company Beevers and Barrett Ltd , of Huddersfield, was bought and in 2004 Samuel Grant (Midlands) came into existence. The Midlands branch was formed to extend the Sheffield arm of the business and when it was closed it was incorporated within the Sheffield branch with brand new premises built to accommodate both sites.

Above: David Grant with a portrait of his grandfather.

The Leeds conversion floor closed after the decision was made to outsource sheeting, reeling and guillotining and the North West branch followed suit after the collapse of its biggest customer, the Ilford photographic company.

In 2005, after 46 years managing the company, David Grant retired. He could look back with pride at a business that he had grown from a small schools' equipment and tailor's consumables company into the leading packaging manufacturer in the North of England. On his retirement, Andrew and Matthew took over as joint managing directors. A year later CL Plastics was sold as a going concern but with the premises and buildings retained under Grant's ownership.

In 2008 Samuel Grant Group was officially incorporated as the business continued to grow. Marmax took over the entire Stanley site while Samuel Grant (North East) relocated to Jarrow and 5-Star Packaging's stock was bought.

Marmax's Matthew Grant landed the biggest single order - £1.8 million - in Samuel Grant Group's history when it was given the job of replacing all Morrison's wooden boxes with recycled plastic ones.

Meanwhile, the Leeds trade counter opened. Other purchases included Clean Solutions North East's order book, steel strapping company Centerpac Ltd's order book and fixtures, and Able Pharmaceutical Packaging, Cheshire.

The next few years would see a great deal of activity culminating in the construction of a 50,000 sq ft warehouse at the Leeds City Enterprise Zone at Thornes Farm.

Left: Making a Marmax heavy duty picnic bench in September, 2008.

Above: The staff at Samuel Grant Packaging at the official opening of their new Leeds headquarters in 2015. **Below left:** The ribbon cutting at the opening of the new premises, featuring the next generation of Grants - the four great great grandsons of Samuel Grant.

The opening of the new warehouse was a memorable occasion and very much a family affair. The opening ceremony ribbon was cut by Samuel Grant's four great great grandsons. Fraser Grant (8) spoke with pride about how his great great grandfather, Samuel, started the business in 1891.

More than 100 staff, contributors and local supporters celebrated the opening of the warehouse which will allow Grant's, now renamed and rebranded as Samuel Grant Packaging, to continue its expansion plans.

Andrew and Matthew Grant have continued the company's carefully thought out policy of prudent expansion. "Being family run has allowed us to grow in a steady way with a strategic plan," he said.

It's a plan that clearly works. As Samuel Grant Packaging prepares to celebrate its 125th anniversary this latest - and biggest - investment will allow the company to develop key areas of the business and to continue to be at the forefront of providing innovative packaging solutions.

Above: Matthew and Andrew Grant cutting the first sod on the warehouse site in November, 2014.

Schneider Electric
The power to make a difference

Schneider Electric is the global specialist in energy management and automation. With global revenues of €25 billion - almost £20 billion - in 2014, its 170,000 employees serve customers in over 100 countries, helping them to manage their energy and process in ways that are safe, reliable, efficient and sustainable. From the simplest of switches to complex operational systems, Schneider technology, software and services improve the way its customers manage and automate their operations.

Schneider Electric has grown through investment and acquisitions of companies who are able to support and enhance its core offer. And it is through such acquisitions that a company formed by two brothers in France in the early 19th century eventually came to Leeds.

The company's origins in Leeds can be traced back to one man, W.H. Turner, whose success in a national engineering competition put into motion a chain of events that eventually led to Schneider Electric purchasing a company called The Yorkshire Switchgear Group and bringing this French engineering giant to Leeds.

Above: Schneider Electric HQ "Le Hive" in Paris, France.

Turner's design of equipment, which allowed the tram driver to change the points ahead, without stopping, was chosen as the competition winner. As a result, on June 11th, 1907, "Tramway Supplies Ltd." was founded by Messrs. Turner, Dixon and Lawton, and the patented 'Turner Automatic Point Controller' soon became a standard feature on electric tramways throughout the world.

Originally the company rented premises from S. Dixon and Sons Ltd in Swinegate, close to what is today the Queens Hall, and at some stage in those formative years also occupied garage premises around Blenheim Terrace, adjacent to Leeds University.

Even in those early days, the company's product range was already expanding. In addition to manufacturing specifically tramway equipment, the company manufactured switchgear and fusegear to control the power supply to the tram wires. As demand for electricity supply increased in the early part of the century, overhead lines began to spread all over the country and a growing demand for switchgear to control the network developed. As a result Tramway Supplies began to invest in developing this technology and switchgear gradually became the company's most important product area.

In 1919, in anticipation of a further post-war expansion of business, the company moved to a site on Meanwood Road which offered room for future development. In 1925, as switchgear products increasingly dominated the company's activities, it changed its name to Yorkshire Switchgear.

Above: An aerial photograph showing Schneider Electric manufacturing facility in Hunslet when it opened in 1998.

Tramway Supplies Ltd

The City of Leeds was the first city in England to install an electric tramway supplied from an overhead system, and was therefore an obvious location for the establishment of a company to manufacture the various types of equipment required.

Above: High voltage equipment used for testing products at Yorkshire Switchgear pictured in the 1930s. *Below:* An aerial photograph showing Yorkshire Switchgear works, formerly located adjacent to Meanwood Cricket Club on Meanwood Road.

Yorkshire Switchgear

The Yorkshire Switchgear group was an international organisation which manufactured electrical switchgear, fusegear, controlgear and transformers for the industries and public utilities of the world.

From its beginnings in the early part of the 20th century, the group eventually comprised Yorkshire Switchgear, EMMCo. Switchgear, the L.V. Division based in Scarborough, and Lindley Thompson, a manufacturer of electrical transformers based in Slough. Overseas, the group operated subsidiaries in Australia, New Zealand, South Africa and Singapore, as well as a worldwide network of agents.

It was during the Second World War, when production at the Leeds factory was switched entirely to the manufacture of power units for radar sets, that EMMCo. was born. Because it was feared that Leeds, as an industrial area, might be heavily bombed, the Government required that production facilities be duplicated in a 'safe area'. As a result, the Electro-Mechanical Manufacturing Co. Ltd. (EMMCo.) began manufacturing in Scarborough on Monday, July 29th, 1943. Today, the Scarborough site still exists

Above: Inverted Vertical Isolation (IVI) oil circuit breakers, the principal product sold by Yorkshire Switchgear until the early 1970s.

albeit under the Schneider Electric name, producing low-voltage switchgear for a variety of clients including the U.K's electrical distribution utilities.

After the war, Yorkshire Switchgear established strong contacts with Shell Petroleum, who as part of their post-war redevelopment had decided to re-equip their refineries across the world. This brought in business from countries such as Venezuela, Aden, Indonesia and Columbia and took a very large percentage of the Leeds factory's production in the immediate post-war years.

A significant date in the newly-named company's history was 1938, when the late George Caton joined the organisation as technical director and introduced his patented Inverted Vertical Isolation (IVI) design of oil circuit breaker. While development and marketing of the IVI was suspended by the switch in production during World War Two, the unit soon became the company's principal product and remained so until the early 1970s.

In 1952 the introduction of the Tyke ring main unit, which was developed from IVI technology and successfully incorporated three switches in a single tank, assured the group's leading position in the electricity distribution business.

Changing market demands linked together with new technology resulted in the introduction in the early 1970s of the 'SQ-HI' range of oil circuit breakers, oil switches and fuse switches.

By the late 1970s it was evident that the electricity supply industry was having new thoughts on its future requirements. As a direct consequence the company embarked on an extensive research and development programme. Yorkshire Switchgear chose to put its faith in sulphur hexafluoride (SF6) technology, an electrical-arc extinguishing gas which had been successfully employed at transmission voltages for many years and is still widely used to this day.

The YSF6 circuit breaker was launched at the Hanover Fair in 1981 and within the first year of its launch, it was credited with a merit award for technical excellence at Electrex 1982.

The company followed up its successful circuit-breaker by applying the new technology to developing a new unit for electrical distribution applications. In 1987, Yorkshire Switchgear launched the SF Ringmaster ring main unit, a groundbreaking innovation consisting of two switches and a circuit breaker contained within

Above: Yorkshire Switchgear welcome new senior management from Merlin Gerin with a Bastille Day Lunch in Leeds.

one SF6-filled tank. A variety of this, the Ringmaster RN2c, is still manufactured in large quantities in the Leeds factory today.

It has enjoyed a market-leading position for many years in the UK, as well as being successfully exported overseas to clients in Africa, Asia, Australasia, India and the Americas. This product has been arguably the biggest success story of Schneider Electric in the UK and you can be certain that there is a good chance that the substation supplying power to your home as you read this will contain a Ringmaster product.

The group, while being fiercely proud of its history of independence, decided in early 1988 to join together with Merlin Gerin, the electrical distribution arm of French electrical engineering giant Schneider Electric, and became a wholly-owned subsidiary of that group.

Schneider Electric

From 1836 to today, Schneider Electric has transformed itself into the global specialist in energy management. Starting from its roots in

Right: Senior managers of Schneider Electric and local dignitaries formally open the new manufacturing facility in 1998. *Inset:* The state-of-the-art Schneider Electric manufacturing facility in Hunslet.

Above: Merlin Gerin Yorkshire Switchgear staff celebrate the French connection and Channel Tunnel order with a float at the Lord Mayor's Parade in 1993.

the iron and steel industry, heavy machinery and shipbuilding, it moved into electricity and automation management.

After World War II, much like Yorkshire Switchgear in the UK, Schneider in France had to change in order to help rebuild a

nation. The company undertook in-depth restructuring conducted in 1949 to prepare Schneider for the modern world.

Executive Charles Schneider wanted the company to "expand, modernize and rationalize". He applied this slogan to all the business segments, from construction and steel to electricity and nuclear power, as well as to Schneider's strategy of acquisitions and exports. Charles' policy met with great success, and in 1959, General de Gaulle declared that Schneider was "leading the national economy".

Merlin Gerin was brought into the group in 1986 and this heralded an ambitious acquisitions strategy, including the integration of Telemecanique, Square D and of course, Yorkshire Switchgear Group.

Yorkshire Switchgear's Meanwood HQ soon had a new sign above the door, "Merlin Gerin Yorkshire Switchgear". The company was then renamed Schneider Electric UK Ltd in 1992 as part of the group's consolidation of its many disparate brands and trading names.

Above: The Hunslet Engine Works office building, now Grade II listed and incorporated into the Schneider Electric facility on Jack Lane. **Left:** A blue plaque awarded in 1995 to signify historical significance of the site as former home of Hunslet Engine Company.

Being part of a much larger group has enabled a company with humble beginnings to invest and grow as a business and in 1998 it was able to build state-of-the-art manufacturing facilities at Jack Lane in Hunslet, Leeds. The building itself covers 17,000 sq m and is one of the largest manufacturing facilities in the city. It is situated in an area covering a total of 40,000 sq m including production lines, stores, offices, car parking and outdoor storage areas.

Products manufactured at the site include high voltage switchgear and transformers as well as adapting imported offers from other Schneider Electric facilities overseas for use in the UK market. Schneider Electric products manufactured in Leeds can be found all over the UK and indeed the world; from the substations powering our homes and businesses, to oil rigs, wind farms, nuclear power stations and football stadia.

Left: Hunslet Engine Co. offices on Jack Lane pictured before making way for the new Schneider Electric facility.

Hunslet Engine Works and Middleton Railway

Approaching the Schneider Electric factory it is clear to see that the site has a rich heritage. There may be modern offices and production lines but the English Heritage blue plaque on the brick building adjacent to Jack Lane and the tracks still crossing the road give an indication of the manufacturing history of this site as the former home of Hunslet Engine Works. The Hunslet Engine Company was founded in 1864 and manufactured steam-powered shunting locomotives on the site for over 100 years.

The company's first steam locomotive was built in 1865 - a standard gauge 0-6-0ST delivered to Thomas Brassey at Ampthill in Bedfordshire for use during construction of the Midland Railway. The 150th anniversary of Hunslet's first locomotive being produced was marked by the Middleton Railway – located in South Leeds close to the Hunslet hotbed of locomotive construction - over July 18-19 2015.

During the celebration steam was returned to the Jack Lane site, once the location of Hunslet's works. Middleton Railway operated two parallel 2ft gauge tracks in what is now the Schneider Electric car park and enabled a probable once in a lifetime opportunity to see two locomotives in steam at the historic location.

Locomotives in operation over the weekend included Trangkil No. 4 - the last steam locomotive to be built at the Jack Lane works – and Irish Mail. Once of the Dinorwic slate quarry in North Wales, Irish Mail represents the iconic 'Quarry Hunslet' type produced by Hunslet.

Schneider Electric is proud to be associated with such an important local and global name as Hunslet Engine Works and were delighted to be able to support Middleton Railway as they celebrated an important milestone for the company.

Left: Steam locomotives return to Jack Lane in July 2015 as part of Hunslet 150 Celebrations.

Middleton Railway

Middleton Railway is the world's oldest working railway. It can trace its origins back to a waggonway built around 1755, followed by a more direct line authorised by a 1758 Act of Parliament. Steam locomotives were introduced in 1812, enabling the railway to claim it provided the first regular revenue earning use of steam traction, as opposed to experimental operation. These locomotives employed a rack and pinion drive on one side and the line's gauge was actually 4ft 1in. The system was converted to standard gauge in 1881.

In 1959 Middleton became the first standard gauge preservation scheme in the country. Today it is run entirely by volunteers, who operate train services (mainly at weekends) between Moor Road station and Middleton Park, in south Leeds. Also on site is a shop that sells souvenirs, sweets and hot and cold drinks. Also, an extensive museum collection is on display in the Engine House and entry to this is free.

Left: The impressive museum collection, which consists of many items from the history of the railway and of the Leeds locomotive building industry. Below: A steam train picking up passengers at Moor Road.

Above: Painting of the façade of the Hunslet Road offices built in 1911. In the corner is the original entrance for the steel delivered by horse and cart from Leeds Station. The canteen (right) was completed in 1917.

T.F. & J.H. Braime
Keeping the wheels turning

The Braime engineering business, situated on Hunslet Road, Leeds, was built on the mass manufacture of oil cans. An oil can is now an almost redundant hand tool but in the 19th and early 20th Century it was in as common usage as a computer today. At that time all machinery, whether in a factory or being used as a means of transport, had to be lubricated by hand.

Braime was not the only manufacturer of oil cans in the UK but it became the most famous. A number of unique features were patented and, ultimately, Braime invented the first "force feed" oil can, including its own pump. Models in steel or brass were widely

Above: An early advertisement for the force feed oil can.

sold throughout Europe, and the Braime can was also adopted by the British Navy, and by merchant fleets at home and abroad. Oilcan manufacture was done in two attic workshops running back above the central office block.

Millions of cans were exported to Europe and to places as far apart as Argentina and Russia, Australia, India and South Africa, where they were selected as the standard "oiler" for their expanding railway industries and were supplied badged with their own company brass label. The railway model of the Braime

Above: Presentation of long service awards by the founder, Tom Braime (left). The event included the quality check of the oil can exported to railway companies worldwide.

oil can, with its long spout, is often seen in films set in the era of the steam engine, being used to oil the large locomotive wheels.

The business was founded in 1888 by Tom Braime, a young apprentice trained engineer, from Rothwell. His father, George, had been the first of the family to go to university in Edinburgh and had become the village vet - previous generations had been the blacksmiths in Barwick-in-Elmet.

Tom returned to his family roots in the metal industry and was apprenticed at McLaren's, before moving to Fowler's, the famous Leeds manufacturer of mobile steam tractors. He quickly became responsible for delivering and commissioning these early workhorses of the Industrial Revolution before deciding at a young age to start his own business in a rented room over a tannery in Leake Street, making and selling the oil cans he had used in his previous employment.

Tom's business expanded rapidly and he moved to larger premises, first in Glasshouse Street, and then to Donisthorpe Street. Tom was joined by his younger brother, Harry, who proved to be an equally inventive engineer. Much later, the name of the company was changed to T.F & J.H Braime.

Above: *Typical products made by Deep Drawn Pressing.*

In the early 1900s the brothers were pioneers of the new technology of deep drawn pressing. Previously, metal had been hammered to shape in the blacksmith's forge, cast as molten metal, bent, spun or rolled and joined by riveting or welding. The entirely new process of deep drawn pressing involved trapping a flat sheet of ductile steel between a top and bottom die, before the male die was driven mechanically into the female die. Under the extreme pressure, the metal was forced to flow into the narrow gap between the two tools through a process called the plastic deformation of the steel. The resulting container was formed without seams and this offered a huge opportunity for the first mass production of items as diverse as kitchen sinks and parts for the nascent motor industry.

Below: *A view of the original jobbing layout of the main press shops.*

In 1909, without any financial resources of their own, the two brothers raised the capital they needed by means of a public loan to buy a four-and-a-half acre site adjacent to Hunslet Road, including a foundry and former brush factory on Brookfield Street and extending across farmland to Sayner Road.

The new imposing offices and factory were built in Edwardian style in brick and stained glass and designed and built by the brothers and their own workforce. The new factory was a statement of their ambition for the business, which had grown from one employee, the founder, to more than a thousand, in less than 25 years.

The very high central bays were built to house a rolling mill to make the special steel that they required – but when the First World War broke out in 1914 the plans were shelved and the steel continued to come to Leeds Station by rail from South Wales and then by horse-drawn wagon through the ornate corner arch still visible from Hunslet Road.

The brothers also designed and built the new special machines they needed. Each was individually named; the largest of which, a triple action 600 tonne press, named "Napoleon", is exhibited just inside the entrance to the factory. All the machinery was positioned in lines either side of the three long central workshops. Each machine was individually belt-driven from a long line shaft, powered by a single engine, a system which minimised power consumption.

The company became a "jobbing press shop", making in batches hundreds of different parts for a large number of customers. Each part required its own different sequence of operations and was transferred manually between machines. Both the jobbing nature of the business and the layout of production can be seen from the early photograph of the main press shops. Despite the introduction of more modern presses - a process started in the 1970s by Ronnie Braime, Harry Braine's only son - the manufacturing process remained largely unchanged for nearly 90 years.

Above: 'Napoleon', the company's oldest press.

Tom and Harry Braime invented and patented a large number of items, from a simple pie dish with a non-drip flange, to very deep sealable waste commodes, which were exported to countries lacking a sewage system.

During the First World War the factory made munitions, including naval sea mines, made out of two pressed hemispheres, and toggled and seamed in the same way that they had made steel floats for the fishing industry in peace time. A photograph in the current offices shows a display of the different sizes of mines with the disturbing graphic "The Tree of Death".

The brothers' most important contribution was the invention of a new process, displayed in the Industrial War Museum, for making the rifling bands needed to maintain the trajectory of all shells from small army cannon to the 18-inch diameter shells fired by battleships. The demand

Left: Key staff from Braime Pressings in 1993 receiving a 'Preferred Supplier' award from a major customer in the automotive industry.

for shells far outstripped the limited capacity in the UK for the traditional method of manufacturing the rifle bands so Braime's invented a new process. Starting with a large flat circular blank of Brass, they drew a shallow pressing. They then punched out the center, leaving an L-shaped ring of brass, which was driven onto the body of the casing of an 18-inch shell.

The process was then repeated using the 18-inch centre punching to create the band for the 16-inch shell. This process was repeated over again to make the rifle band for the next size of shell, ultimately achieving almost 100 per cent usage of the valuable material. For this invention, one of the brothers was awarded an OBE but refused it because he felt the award should have been offered to both of them.

During the war, Harry Braime burnt himself out working night and day, rarely returning to his new home in Chapeltown. Shortly after the end of the war, he suddenly left the business and his only son, Ronald, had to leave university early to take over production. Henry never returned to work and died at an early age. However, Tom, the original founder, worked into his 70s, became well-known in the city, was a founder of Moortown Golf Club, and lived to be 94.

During the war, large numbers of male employees, including the only son of Tom Braime, enlisted in the Yorkshire Regiments. Their names are recorded on a memorial in the canteen. The majority lost their lives in France or Flanders.

By 1917, the company was employing over 500 women and the founders built a canteen to provide them with hot meals. The canteen, opened by Princess Mary, was the first in Leeds and reputedly the first in the UK. It was built with a level of luxury not available to employees at home. The canteen stands as a monument to one of the few social benefits of the First World War, the emancipation of working women, who were allowed to do work previously reserved for men.

Above: The elevator belt storage area. ***Above left:*** The 'Watchdog' is the company's signature product for monitoring the production of bucket elevators and conveyors, first launched in 1985. ***Below:*** The new high storage area for buckets.

Above: A press making filter cans.

Above: A belt drilling machine.

The canteen was still of its time - the men and women were segregated on different floors either by accident or design, and the women's canteen was above.

The company survived the challenges of the Depressions that followed both wars - and also the Great Depression of 1929 and the boom and busts of the 1980s. However, by the start of the current century, the majority of its customers had either failed or been taken over by overseas conglomerates, who had relocated their manufacturing outside of the UK.

To survive, Braime Pressings has totally changed its type of manufacture to cellular format, using robotic or automated transfer presses, and now specialises in producing very large volumes of a limited range of components for a small customer base. This change is reflected in the current layout of the factory. The workforce has reduced to about 40 but with a much higher skill base, largely producing enclosures for disposable filters, rather than the original oilcans with their patented Grit Excluder, the product on which the business was founded.

Another group of products manufactured by Braime's from about 1900 were seamless steel elevator buckets. Braime was the first company to make these products as deep drawn pressings and by 1905 the company sales brochures detail a range of 500 sizes. Starting in the 1970s, Braime's began to export increasing quantities of new versions of this niche product, first to Europe and then further afield.

Bucket elevators are used to convey granular

Right: Managing Director Nicholas Braime.

material, like cereals, vertically into or out of storage or used in the processing of materials for the manufacture of product such as beer, whisky, edible oils, food, flour and animal feed, or in the manufacture of industrial products, for example, glass bottles, cement, or Aggregates. At one end of the scale, they are used by farmers to lift small tonnages of grains by say 15 metres to feed grain driers. At the other end of the scale, the product is used to elevate up to 2,000 tonnes per hour and to heights of 80 metres in a grain terminal or oil processor.

Braime's designed and patented improved versions of the buckets and developed their own bespoke software to enable them to advise customers on how to optimise the efficiency of the elevator – and, ultimately, the design parameters of the machine itself.

Subsequently, Braime's added the manufacture of the special elevator bolts and the distribution of elevator belts and the manufacture of heavy duty chain to transport the same materials through horizontal conveyors running above or below the storage silos.

From the early 1980s, Braime's developed electronic sensors and systems to reduce the very real risk of serious fires and explosions when handling flammable products, like grain, in high volumes. Braime's has become the market leader in this field.

More recently the company has started to produce systems to provide preventative maintenance

Above: Gas canisters made by the company.

Above: A modern, automated cell for manufacturing high volume components.

throughout large storage and processing facilities. These specialised products for the material handling industry are sold under the brand "4B" – better buckets, bolts and belts. Today, the company has overseas subsidiaries or offices in the UK, France, Germany, Thailand, the USA, South Africa and Australia and sells to a further 50 countries through a network of d1istributors.

In 1950, the company was floated on the London Stock Exchange and has more recently moved to the "AIM" market. Today the company management includes the grandson and great grandsons of Harry Braime. The company continues to be supported by its shareholders, many of whom are descendants of either Tom and Harry Braime.

In 2015, the company sold 25% of its site to the Government and the funds from the sale are being used to modernise the remainder of the facility. The area sold will become the first University Technical College for Leeds and provide 600 students with a technical based curriculum, enabling them either to go on to university or to take up places as apprentices, where they can continue their higher education while in paid employment.

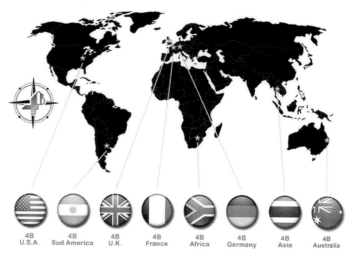

| 4B U.S.A. | 4B Sud America | 4B U.K. | 4B France | 4B Africa | 4B Germany | 4B Asia | 4B Australia |

Above: A map of the 4B subsidiaries spread across the continents.

ingenuity and determination to call upon, will prove to be an inspiration and an example of what can be achieved by a career in engineering.

Hopefully, being educated side by side with a successful and historic engineering business, founded by two young entrepreneurs with nothing but their

Right: An impression of the exterior of the University Technical College being built within the original Braime factory.

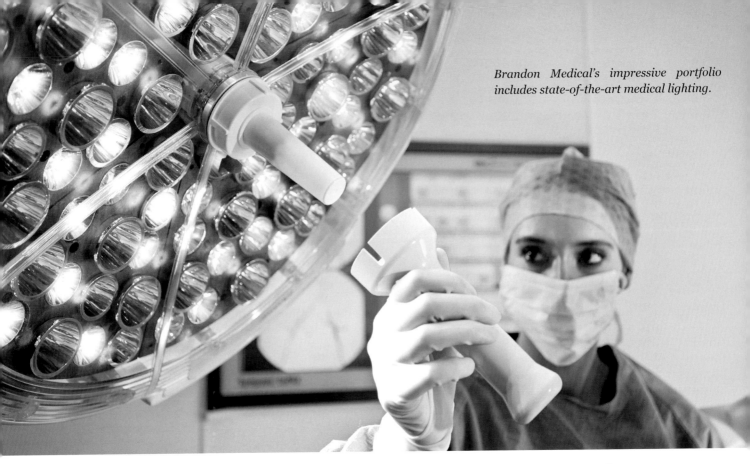

Brandon Medical's impressive portfolio includes state-of-the-art medical lighting.

Brandon Medical
A shining light in health care

It is not usually a welcome experience to find yourself in hospital, but if the situation arises then patients need to know that everything possible is being done for them.

They may not realise it, but there is a company with some 65 years' experience that has been providing the world of health care with first rate support for an element of that time. Most of us would regard assistance in a hospital as meaning something to do with the medicines or potions that help out the professionals who treat us. However, Brandon Medical Ltd offers something else. It is a company that literally throws light on an operation.

If you were in a hospital theatre where a surgeon was carrying out work with scalpel and sutures, then having a clearly lit arena would be very important for all concerned. That is where this company comes in with its wide range of operating theatre

lamps, as well as an array of supporting hardware such as audio-visual systems, lighting panels, close quarter lighting and more intimate examination lights.

The company began life just after the last war as a motor rewind firm, before progressing into transformer manufacture. It was founded by Joseph Cameron and son Cyril, with much of the work at the time being contract based. In the earlier days, a small part of the work involved making medical equipment such as the dramatically named Sharman Portable Kymographic Tubal Insufflation Apparatus.

This machine was used in sterility clinics, but further

Left: *Adrian and Graeme Hall examine a piece of surgical lighting equipment. The two brothers developed Brandon Medical with the financial and commercial expertise of their father, Eric.*

detail than that is not required here. The company also developed something called a Snow Pencil that involved using a tube powered by a CO_2 Sparklets bulb to eradicate skin blemishes. However, it was the firm's development of the Oxford Speclite that helped encourage it to move into the production of medical lighting supplies in a big way.

The Speclite was originally produced at the instigation of the Oxford Hospital Board and was designed to provide the facilities for visually examining infusion fluids in glass or plastic containers. By then, Graeme Hall, with the assistance of his father, had taken over the ailing Brandon Engineering Ltd, gaining control in 1993 and turning it into Brandon Medical. Included in the workforce was a certain Alan Portrey, an employee who would complete 40 years' service in 2014. He was just one of the original factory staff who were regarded as very important by the new owners in maintaining production standards and in developing the business along new lines. The Halls were joined by Graeme's brother, Adrian, in 1995 as the company was stabilised and basic systems for quality and management introduced.

By now, as Brandon Medical, the firm was successful in winning two SMART awards that helped fund new technological development that led to the production of the Galaxy Ultra range of operating lights. The formal rebranding from an engineering concern to a medical devices' company was completed in 1996. The following year saw Graeme win a major Manufacturing Managers' award for rescuing the Brandon business and Adrian was at the forefront in leading a consortium that won the contract to rebuild hospitals in Bosnia.

The company was going from strength to strength and the century was coming to an end as the Halls secured their biggest ever single order when supplying the operating theatre control panels in the internationally renowned King Abdullah Hospital near Ar Ramtha, Jordan. Further awards for its optical systems for operating lights were to follow and a new series of Galaxy mobile operating lights were introduced in 2004.

About the same time, Brandon brought out an expanded range of Coolview examination lights, the Amadea bed-head lamps and a new set of UPS units. This was now a company firmly established as a major player in its field, having also benefited from a move to new premises a year into the present century. A new design lab was then added and staff appointed to integrate aesthetic considerations with the practicality and efficiency of the products being manufactured.

In 2005, the first version of a video system was launched. This would lead to the development

Above: The Hall family – Eric, Adrian Mary and Graeme in the demonstration theatre.

of Symposia, a digital media communication package designed specifically for healthcare. The first major installation of Symposia occurred at Liverpool University.

Closer to home, the Seacroft Hospital makes important use of a Brandon product. The hospital is the largest NHS based IVF facility in the country and a specially designed embryo cell safety light was designed for use here. Visible blue light is harmful to certain embryonic cells, but Brandon was able to come up with a high definition LED spectrum light source that filtered out dangerous wavelengths, resulting in a cell safe light that eliminated the danger of 'blue light toxicity'. Not surprisingly, this innovation meant that the company was given the coveted European Elektra Award in 2009.

By now the Brandon name was so well known that the company was approached by Sony to act as a 'dealer' for its healthcare

Below: Adrian Hall at the British Embassy in Sarajevo soon after it opened after the end of hostilities. Brandon Medical held talks at the embassy on the best way to co-operate with the Ministry of Health in Bosnia to refit 13 hospitals in Bosnia after the company had won an international tender.

products and a deal was struck that resulted in the supply of medical monitors, printers, recorders and a variety of other peripherals and consumables. Further awards came the company's way, including the immensely prestigious 2011 Queen's Award for Enterprise in the Innovation Category. Further expansion of the product range of HD-LED equipment helped push forward the need to move home again. So, in 2013, Brandon Medical moved to a state of the art site in Morley where it could now double its operating capacity.

It now introduced the Quasar eLite, an advanced operating theatre light system that produces an unrivalled picture quality on large monitors. The new premises were officially opened on July 9th, 2014, by the Princess Royal, a sure sign of the standing to which Brandon Medical had risen.

The company can be said to be on a mission in that it wants its clients to regard it as being the first port of call when looking for a supplier to meet their needs. To this end, it aims to provide desirable, innovative and high value products, but ones that are not delivered in a cold, impersonal manner. The 'hands-on' service has always been important and has helped establish a reputation as a business that supplies an after sales service that is just as important as that delivered at the front end of a deal. It is not just the product that is of concern, because Brandon sees itself as also offering support to medical staff, healthcare engineers and distributors in delivering a better patient care package. In addition, a large number of veterinary practices and animal sanctuaries rely on Brandon lighting in their surgeries, laboratories and medical rooms.

The company does not just deliver and install its equipment as it also ensures that customers are given appropriate training and education to assist them carry out their work

Above: The Lord Lieutenant of West Yorkshire, Dr Ingrid Roscoe, present the Queen's Award at Brandon Medical HQ. *Below:* Adrian meets the Queen when Brandon Medical received the Queen's Award for Innovation in 2011.

to the highest possible standards. There is an ethical element to all this as Brandon holds with so-called old fashioned values of integrity and honesty, whilst all the time regarding customers and clients as partners.

Doing things in hospital the Brandon way has meant considerable changes to the concept the general public once had of the way in which teaching hospitals work. People brought up on 'Emergency Ward 10' might still imagine that students learn by watching surgeons and then practising what they have observed on live patients! That process has long been consigned to history as now trainee doctors can follow everything from a safe uncontaminated distance, but thanks to our modern digital world everything is integrated into a system. This enables observation from a safe, remote place, but it appears to those watching that they are at the surgeon's elbow.

Brandon Medical had a turnover of £500,000 in 1993, but this has risen to over £5 million today and is still growing. The Hall brothers, now co-managing directors, have bold ambitions to quadruple the company in size by the early 2020s and are planning steady development in Far East markets. Closer to home, keep an eye out for its lights as used in operating theatres and medical centres in TV and movie dramas. The sets have to be realistic and what better way is there of achieving this realism than by using the best form of lighting to be had?

Above: Brandon Medical's impressive new headquarters opened in 2014.

'Brilliant by design' is the Brandon slogan and one that is reflected in every aspect of its being.

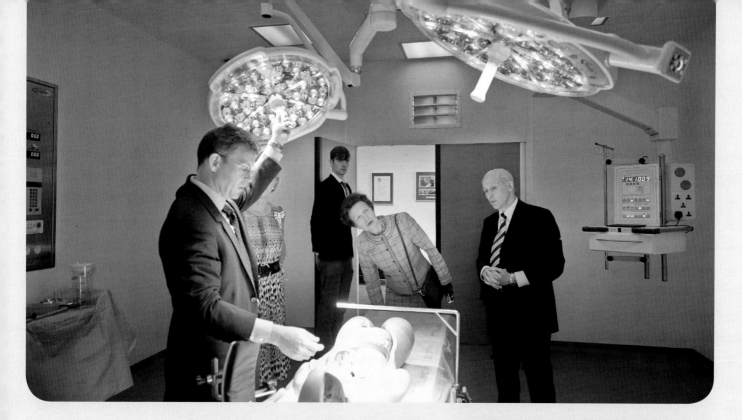

HRH The Princess Royal visited Brandon Medical in July, 2014. The visit marked the official opening of the company's new premises in Morley - a facility which has more than doubled its operating capacity.

The Princess was invited to try out Brandon's impressive portfolio of products in the state-of-the-art visitor centre followed by a tour of the factory and the unveiling of a plaque. It was the second royal honour for Brandon Medical. In 2011, the company received the Queen's award for Enterprise in the Innovation Category, possibly the most prestigious award possible in its field.

Brandon Medical Company Limited

OPENED BY

HRH The Princess Royal

ON 9TH JULY 2014

● European
○ Business
○ Awards

Geo. Spence and Sons Ltd

Ironmongers span the generations

It started as a one-man business and grew to become one of Leeds' best-known ironmongers selling everything from locks to ladders, power tools to protective clothing. George Spence and Sons was established more than 120 years ago and remains a family business today.

George Spence was a highly respected leather merchant who started a business with his wife, Sarah, in the late 1880s from a small shop in West Street, Leeds. As more stock was added to an already comprehensive range, the business outgrew its premises and moved to 52, Wellington Road next to the North Eastern Gas Board's town gas plant.

Another shop was opened at 55, Beeston Road where George, with wife Sarah, and sons Sydney, Frederick and Rowland, made their home. Sarah ran the Beeston Road business while George took care of the Wellington Road store. When he became old enough, Sydney worked in the business until he joined the Army at the start of the First World War.

Top: *The impressive store operated by the Spence family at 52-56, Wellington Road.* **Left:** *The Spence family takes to the road in this early photograph, from left, George and Sarah with children Sydney, Frederick and Rowland.*

With Sydney away, Frederick left school at the age of 14 to help in the Wellington Road shop.

When Sydney returned from war duty he took over the running of the Beeston Road shop which he continued to manage until it was earmarked for demolition in the 1960s.

Meanwhile, youngest son, known as Rowley, joined the expanding business in the early 1920s and three years later plans were approved for alterations and additions to 52 and 54, Wellington Road. Plans included a second floor above the single-storey buildings which almost doubled the working area.

Frederick's daughter, Maureen, vividly remembers visiting 52, Wellington Road and seeing a hole in the ceiling which enabled leather to be hoisted to the second floor some 14ft up and protected by a simple, single bar to prevent anyone from falling through. Clearly, health and safety regulations were not as rigorous back then!

It was around this time that George invented and began making 'Toppa' metal boot protectors which were in demand all over the country. A later development was the 'Neeto' leather boot protector which featured on the business's advertising material.

Between the First and Second World Wars Rowley opened a shop at 388-390 Dewsbury Road. When war broke out in 1939 he was stationed at Burtonwood, a US air force base near Warrington, Lancashire.

Frederick continued to run the Wellington Road shop during the day while working at night as a volunteer ambulance driver. One of his regular tasks was collecting the wounded from Leeds railway station and taking them to local hospitals including St James's and Meanwood.

Left: George Spence in 1936.

The firm played its part in the war effort by making articles for the American Air Force. Because of their knowledge of leather work they were asked to make protective gaiters for use in Flying Fortress aircraft. The company had a Ministry licence to obtain the specially treated freeze-proof leather required.

Some of this work was done in the workshop at Wellington Road while George, now in his 70s, worked on the dining room table punching the holes for laces. Not long after, George, then 75, handed the business over to his sons.

After the war the shoe repair trade declined and the firm had to adapt to the many changes taking place by developing the tool supply side of the business.

In 1951, the business became a limited company – Geo. Spence and Sons Ltd. The decade saw a gradual diversification into ironmongery and electrical goods followed by a range of do-it-yourself products.

During the 50s and 60s the business had an established delivery round covering Leeds and surrounding towns servicing the shoe repair trade.

The shop was extended by knocking through and incorporating the ground floor of 54, Wellington Road, previously a butcher's.

In the mid-50s Frederick's son-in-law, Alan Ball, joined the company followed in 1961 by Frederick's son, Terence, then 16, after completing his RSA exams.

With the soaring interest in DIY came the introduction of materials such as hardboard, plywood

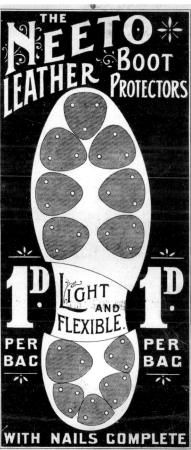

Above: Advertising Neeto leather boot protectors at one penny a bag.

Above: A steam tram featuring an advertisement for Geo Spence.

and beadings. The fashion for flush doors made sheets of hardboard and matching beadings major sellers. Along with flush doors, people were also fitting ball catches and pull handles.

Pearl effect door handles were popular and hundreds were sold.

Paraffin heaters were also in demand and the company had a 600-gallon tank installed at the back of 54, Wellington Road to house paraffin which was sold at the shop and also delivered.

In the early 1960s the shop was knocked through into 56, Wellington Road, formerly a shoe repairers. The company now occupied the whole block between Renton Street and Langham Street including two cottages which were attached to no.56 and used to store bulky items such as bags of sand and cement and fence panels.

Fred, Alan and Terry guided the business through into the 80s – Fred was managing director, his wife, Ivah, looked after all the administration while Alan was manager and ran the day-to-day business.

Sydney continued to run his shop at Beeston Road until it was earmarked for demolition in the late 60s. Although this was a separate business it was supported by the family at Wellington Road.

In 1977 the company, now with eight employees, moved into new premises at 105, Wellington Road. The land and property around no.52 had been compulsorily purchased for the building of the Armley Gyratory road system.

By then the leather and grindery side of the business had all but died out and at the new premises only stick-on soles, laces and polishes were sold – even this ended within a few years.

The move to no.105 allowed for a better showroom area to display a range of woodworking machines. There were regular demonstration days so customers could see the machines in action.

The shelving and storage arm of the business continued to grow. The firm even shipped a small unit to a customer who had gone to live in New York. Throughout this time, however, the mainstay of the business was hand tool and ironmongery sales.

Above and inset: *Frederick Spence, who left school at 14 to help in the Wellington Road shop is pictured cutting leather in 1922.*

In the 80s Alan was instrumental in introducing the company's first computerised accounting machine – an Olivetti the size of a desk! Pauline Flockton, Terry's sister-in-law, operated the sales ledger while Terry's wife, Barbara, ran the purchase ledger.

During this time Fred gradually reduced his involvement in the day-to-day running of the business and Alan opted for semi-retirement leaving Terry to continue actively managing the shop.

Fred continued to work part-time until only a month before he died in June, 1990, at the age of 88. Alan decided to retire in 1993 and Barbara became a director.

Barbara and Terry's son, Nicholas, worked for the business for a short time after university, designing the company's promotional material.

During the decade shelving sales declined but the power tool market grew rapidly, creating new opportunities. A mezzanine floor was installed in 2000 allowing more storage space.

Nick Rose joined the company that year as a salesman and was appointed manager in 2005. Managing director Terry Spence reduced his working week to four days with Barbara continuing as director in charge of finance.

By now the product range included ironmongery, hardware, hand tools, power tools, fixings and fasteners. In addition the firm stocks garden tools, industrial clothing, electrical fittings and a range of plumbing hardware.

The mid-2000s saw a decline in business brought about by the recession leading to Terry taking a more active role again.

Meanwhile Nick Spence and his wife, Fiona, moved back to Yorkshire as their son, George, was nearing school age.

Nick returned to the company in 2012 after 13 years as an industrial designer with Dyson, the vacuum cleaner manufacturer, where he rose to the position of Senior Principal Engineer overseeing four teams of designers.

Nick used his engineering skills to analyse the sales, purchasing and stock data and introduced a number of new initatives including increased focus on competitive pricing. He also introduced a monthly promotional leaflet for customers.

The company has returned to growth and Nick was appointed a director in 2013.

Now, in 2015, Terry, aged 70, decided it was time to pass on the baton and Nick was appointed managing director. The year also saw a refurbishment programme put in place with a new shop front and LED lighting recently installed.

Right: Directors Nick, Barbara and Terry Spence.

Above: Geo Spence's showroom at Wellington Road.

Taking stock, Terry says he is delighted that Nick, the fourth generation of the Spence family, is at the helm bringing his business knowledge and technical expertise to the business and continuing the family tradition.

Who knows, he says, perhaps in the future there may be another George in charge at Geo. Spence and Sons Ltd!

Mone Bros
Company's growing reputation

Top: *Blackhill Quarry, with Golden Acre Park in the background.*
Above: *The firm's founders, from left, James Mone, Philip Mone and John Mone. Philip died in January, 2015.*

Celebrations have been going with a bang at Mone Bros as the company marks 50 years in business.

To recognise the event a video has been produced at the company's Blackhill Quarry which reveals some explosive action as more than 20,000 tonnes of rock were detonated uncovering stone that has been deep underground for millions of years (see www.monebros.co.uk).

Quarrying is just one of the many strings to the bow of Mone Bros founded by three brothers – Philip, James and John Mone – at a small shed located at St Bernard Mills, Gildersome. They could not have had any idea at that time how the business would expand over the years but a strong work ethic has reaped dividends. The business has firmly established a growing reputation in the north over the last 50 years.

The company employs over 80 experienced operators and managerial staff and is involved in a wide range of work including wagon and plant hire, quarrying and waste disposal, civil engineering and aggregate recycling. Mone Bros also provides a wide range of services in the field of excavations, demolition and site clearance.

Initially, in 1965, the business specialised in the maintenance and repair of plant equipment and it was not long before the brothers bought their own excavators for hiring. This led on to the purchase of tipper wagons with one of the earliest jobs working on the Leeds inner city ring road. Having their own machinery - bulk earth moving commenced in the early 1970s. The excavation for the foundations of the Yorkshire Electric headquarters in Scarcroft was one of the first contracts.

Mone Bros is still very much a family concern with John and James at the helm and the next generation, Kevin and Phil Mone, who joined in the 1980s, also on the board of directors, along with operations director Steve Horsley, financial director Andrew Slater and transport director Derek Flatters. In the last 10 years family members, Joseph and James Mone Jr, joined the team.

The firm's headquarters in Morley is only a few miles away from where it all started.

It now operates three more sites with quarries at Eggborough near Selby, Bramhope and New Farnley. Quarrying started at Blackhill Quarry, Bramhope, almost 100 years ago and there are large reserves of high quality stone available. Mone Bros acquired the quarry in 1979 and has been developing and upgrading it to the present day.

The sandstone from the quarry was initially used to produce sand and gravel. It went on to produce walling stone and dressers were employed to make products such as fireplaces and window surrounds. Blackhill quarry stone has been used in many major projects such as Blackfriars Bridge over the River Thames, Armley Prison wall and Kirkstall Abbey and museum.

Below: Something to shout about ... Mone Bros workforce celebrate 50 years in business.

Top: Demolition of the Lowfields Stand, Elland Road, in 1992.
Middle: Renewing the soil and underground heating system in 2011 on the Leeds Carnegie Stadium, Headingley pitch. *Above:* James and Philip Mone repairing machinery in the 1960s.

Above: Principals, from left, Phil Mone Jr, John Mone, James Mone and Kevin Mone.

Both landscaping centres at Bramhope and at New Farnley, Leeds, display a vast range of garden products and decorative gravels designed to enable customers to see and touch different products before deciding which to buy.

The Whitehall recycling depot at New Farnley was purchased in the late 1980s and was used mainly for producing recycled construction materials. In 2008, the company started to produce a high quality Type 1 recycled aggregate.

Eggborough Quarry was acquired in 2011. It produces red sand used for utility works backfill and is also an inert landfill site permitted to recycle incoming waste materials.

Back in the mid-80s recycling was not at the forefront of people's minds. Mobile plant was not as suitable or as readily available as it is now. Concrete, brick, tarmacadam and topsoil were rarely segregated and were usually mixed and tipped together in landfill.

The company's move into recycling was a natural step to take - having its own excavators and tipper wagons enabled the firm to supply aggregates to the industry which made good sense.

Because landfill sites are dwindling in number Mone Bros recycling sites have taken on more significance and are at the heart of the company's business operations, overtaking its plant hire and contracts activities.

Above: Demolishing the famous Headingley Pavilion in 2004. Below: Stone from Mone Bros Blackhill quarry has been used to build and extend some of the most attractive landmark buildings in and around Leeds including this one – Crown Point Bridge, Leeds.

As Phil Mone says: "An increase in environmental awareness has also led to the growth in recycling. When you produce high quality aggregates that are stringently tested, utility and civil engineering companies become ever more confident in using recycled materials."

One of the company's recent recycling projects was the demolition of the former Yorkshire Post building in Wellington Street, Leeds. Concrete was crushed and screened for use on roads across the county.

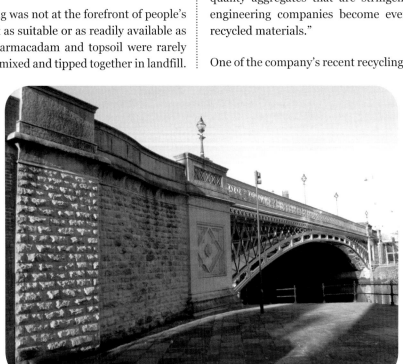

Mone Bros successfully negotiated a passage through the recession with the help of long-standing employees such as Johnny Gallagher, the Oakes brothers, Geoff, Sav and John and Michelle Guy to name just a few, and is now witnessing a real growth in demand from customers and is

working with a growing number of well-known organisations including Northern Gas Networks, Northern Power Grid and Yorkshire Water.

Says John Mone: "We've come a long way since 1965 with the business expanding to where it is now with over 80 staff and an established reputation with major contractors, building firms and homeowners across the Yorkshire region.

"As a business we have gradually diversified over the decades into earth moving, civil engineering, contracting, quarrying, aggregate recycling and retail for gardening and landscaping purposes.

"We have seen many changes in 50 years, not least the transformation of our home city of Leeds into a truly world class

Above: Family business ... John Mone (top left) James Mone (top right), Philip Mone (kneeling), Anthony Mone (left) and Mary Mone (right) with Kevin Mone anxious to get in the picture at St Bernard Mills, Gildersome.

location. We have always stayed true to our family values of honesty, integrity and value and we believe that this philosophy is appreciated by our customers.

"Who knows what the next 50 years will hold for the recycling industry but I am certain that the Mone family will be involved in some way."

Below: Mone Bros' impressive fleet of vehicles.

The Donelec Group
Designs on electronics

When Robert Wheat returned home from the Second World War after serving as a captain in the Royal Mechanical and Electrical Engineers he was determined to pick up the threads of a promising career as a chartered electrical engineer.

He used the experience he had gained to start up in business selling electric heating, lighting and motors from his home.

Within two years this small one-man operation had grown rapidly to become the firm of William Don Ltd with a base at Crown Point Works, Hunslet.

This embryonic company dealt in electric motors and electronically controlled variable speed drives for industrial machinery – the latter a by-product of new technology developed during the war.

William Don Ltd secured an agreement with the firm producing the variable speed drives which gave the company sole selling rights for the north of England. They flew off the shelves!

Robert Wheat and his two partners travelled round the mills and other industrial centres demonstrating how the fingertip speed control given by the electronic valves could increase output and improve quality control. Once the benefits had been illustrated orders were placed and demand for control systems invariably exceeded supply.

Above: Robert Wheat presenting Jack Park with a 25-year long service award. Robert Wheat (centre), Norman Wheat (right) and Jack Park (left). Below: Crown Point.

The solution was for William Don Ltd to move into manufacturing. The company already had a sizeable staff of customer support engineers and technicians who were accustomed to dealing with clients' demands and expectations so the in-house expertise was already in place. What the company didn't have was the room to develop a full-scale control systems manufacturing operation so

relocation was necessary and in 1962 it moved from Hunslet to Kerry Hill, Horsforth.

While the site wasn't ideal, the company enjoyed many successful years there. It branched out into the design and manufacture of its own range of low cost electronic sensing devices for industry and had built a two-storey extension to Kerry Hill Works to accommodate the additional work.

It was around this time that Robert's two sons, Robert and Norman, joined the business. Each in turn had graduated in electrical engineering from Sheffield University. Robert took a graduate apprenticeship while Norman went to America to gain experience.

Above: *Electronics manufacturing at Kerry Hill.*

On completion of his apprenticeship, Robert joined the outside technical sales team at William Don but three years later his career was tragically cut short in a road accident. It fell to Norman to guide the company through the silicon chip revolution.

Don Controls (which formally changed its business name in 1960 to better suit the modern engineering environment), expanded rapidly and landed its first large export contract worth in excess of £100,000. It went on to secure a prestigious contract as systems builders to leading US manufacturer Texas Instruments.

The business's hi-tech team and some office staff moved to a modern building in Low Lane, Horsforth, in 1975 while the Kerry Hill centre was retained for some aspects of production.

The electronics side of Don Controls continued to grow and in

particular a joint venture between Norman Wheat and Nicholas Braime in a microprocessor-based control monitoring system for the grain industry meant it was time to concentrate on both the control panel manufacture as well as the microprocessor based electronic controllers and sensors. To ensure each company was allowed to flourish the electronics side to Don Controls was moved from Low Lane in Leeds to Harrogate under the name of Wheat Electronics, a partnership between Norman and his wife, Patricia.

Right: *Norman Wheat, Managing Director of Don Controls collects the Panel Builder of the Year award in 2000 from Peter Wheeler and Peter Whitfield, both of the IML Group.*

Norman's three sons were now ready to join the business. Jonathan Wheat joined the company after successfully completing his Bachelor of Engineering Honours Degree at Sheffield and introduced the company's first quality system under the BS5750 standard. Richard Wheat joined in 1985 and worked his way through every aspect of the business from warehouse management to panel wiring to purchase control and with David Wheat joining from a six-year stint in the NHS as an accountant, this gave Norman the opportunity to concentrate on the electronics side, ever expanding the range of electronic controllers and sensors.

To help build up the electronics capability of the US company selling the electronic products, Jonathan was based in America to help expand the business which he did very successfully – so much so that he is still working for and running the entire organisation in the US for Don Electronics' main customer. This increase

Above: *Computer aided design in the 1980s.*

in turnover led towards converting the Wheat Electronics partnership between Norman and Patricia into a limited company in 1998.

The new millennium saw two notable successes for Don Controls, firstly it won the prestigious Panel Builder of the Year award and secondly secured its largest ever contract worth £1.5 million from the Leeds based organisation, Schneider Electric. This contract was to build 500 single bay control panels in just eight weeks. In order to achieve this the company lent on the batch manufacturing experience of its sister company and designed a very rapid manufacturing process for the panels including automated testing.

As the electronics arm of the business continued to grow and Don Controls continued its success, it soon became apparent that the current premises in Harrogate were rapidly being outgrown. With this in mind the family made plans to bring back together the two businesses under the one banner, although both keeping their names - The Donelec Group was formed.

The other long term plan was to locate a suitable building to house both businesses. Unfortunately, locating a suitable building proved difficult, especially as the family wanted to keep its roots in the North Leeds area. However, a suitable piece of land was found at the end of the Westfield Industrial Estate, off Kirk Lane in Yeadon and plans were drawn up to build a 40,000 sq ft unit.

The new facility was started in June, 2008, with the plan to build just half the entire building, leaving the second half for phase two.

Above: *The drawing office at the Horsforth site in around 2000.*
Below: *Kerry Hill Works.*

Above: The new building which was completed in May, 2009. **Inset:** *Work in progress in 2008 on a new headquarters off Kirk Lane, Yeadon.*

However, as the order book was growing rapidly, the decision was made to build the whole facility in one go which was completed in April, 2009. This decision proved to be a very sound one as initially it housed the 50 years of paraphernalia that had been collected. Soon demand required more floor space, which fortunately was readily available.

In December, 2014, the Donelec group completed the purchase of Synatel Instrumentation Limited, a manufacturer of controllers and sensors specialising in speed and proximity detection. The company had worked alongside Synatel for many years with both companies supplying the same customer for over 20 years with complimentary electronic equipment. Synatel is being run as an independent business unit for the group but early signs show that both Synatel and Don Electronics will benefit greatly from economies of scales and sharing of good practice.

The group has recently raised a toast to the first employee to reach the 50-year service mark. Ian Hanlon started working for Don Controls aged 15 as an apprentice before

Right: Ian Hanlon (centre), who started work as a 15-year-old apprentice, receives a long service award from David Wheat (left) and Norman Wheat (right).

moving to Harrogate to run the electronics manufacturing side of the business and was now running the electronics production in Yeadon, made this historic achievement without having a single day off for sickness - a truly remarkable achievement.

Norman is now taking a back seat in the running of the companies but is still working on new electronic designs and concepts. The running of the businesses is now down to Richard and David (with support from their wives) who are continuing the family pattern of successfully building on previous generations' work to the extent that Don Controls, Don Electronics and Synatel Instrumentation continued to prosper and grow.

Wilson Power Solutions
Harnessing ways to save energy

From humble beginnings Wilson Power Solutions has grown to be the UK's leading supplier of energy efficient power distribution solutions.

The company manufactures power transformers and helps organisations reduce unnecessary energy wastage to save costs and improve environmental performance.

"We treasure our heritage and know that our hard-earned reputation for service excellence and superior product performance has grown out of 69 years of experience in the power engineering sector," says joint managing director Erika Wilson. "We take great pride in being the preferred and trusted supplier for many of the UK's most successful organisations."

The story of how founder Richard Wilson overcame tragedy in his early life to become one of the north's most respected entrepreneurs is an inspirational one.

Richard's parents died within three months of each other when he was just four years old. He had a brother aged two and a sister who was six months old. The three of them had no less than 23 housekeepers looking after them as they grew up.

Above: *Richard Wilson's first office at Westbourne Place.*

Richard left school at 15 to start an apprenticeship winding motors at Morley Electric, Stanningley. He was made redundant and decided to go it alone. He started his own business rewinding starter motors and dynamos at Westbourne Place in Stanningley, Leeds, mainly for Isles, a local Leyland dealer.

During the Second World War he was requisitioned by Booth's Cranes in Rodley. This crane works is now owned by the company and used as a storage facility.

In 1940 he was transferred to another branch of the Isles business and one assignment he well remembers was when he was asked to work on a top secret job for vehicles destined for the front line in France. When the vehicles arrived they turned out to be 21-year-old Guy lorries with solid tyres – hardly cutting edge motor technology!

Left: *Family business (from left) joint Managing Director, Simon Wilson, Colin Wilson, joint Managing Director Erika Wilson and Dennis Wilson.*

Above: Simon and Erika. ***Inset:*** *Bernard and Richard Wilson (right).*

After the war he returned to his business, now based in Bradford Road, as an auto electrician rewiring vehicles before moving on to electrical contracting.

A trip to a war surplus auction proved fruitful. He went with his friend, George Cohens, who ran a machinery business in Stanningley. Richard bought his first electric motor - which were hard to find at that time - and that marked the start of his used electrical business.

He became an expert in the art of buying and selling. He picked up a consignment of pumping sets which had been used to fill Spitfires at an airfield auction and later sold the lot to the oil industry, no doubt at an acceptable profit!

In 1964 he built King Street Works, Pudsey - 1,200 sq ft of space and fitted with a two-ton electric crane. Two years later he bought part of a foundry on the Grangefield industrial estate doubling the amount of space for storing his growing stock.

In 1967, Richard's two sons, Dennis and Colin, joined to learn the business working on the shop floor overhauling electrical and pumping equipment.

It wasn't all full steam ahead, however. During work to remove valves at Loch Lomond in Scotland the pumping station caught fire and it took the might of the entire Glasgow Fire Service to bring it under control.

Business wasn't easy to come by and Colin took to the road visiting the headquarters of large oil companies and a notable coup was coming away with an order from Texaco to overhaul pumping equipment in the national emergency oil system which was piped around the country.

Meanwhile, Dennis was looking for work as the business was finding it hard to support the three families who depended upon it.

But it's an ill wind and it certainly blew in the right direction during the hardships of the three-day week. Richard spotted an opening and sold a huge quantity of generators and turnover soared six-fold!

He went on to plough back the profits into buying large quantities of motors from gas reforming plants which were closing when North Sea gas came on stream. He moved up a gear and bought larger motors from redundant oil refineries.

149

They increased their stock and invested carefully in the business buying their first mobile crane and high voltage transformer and switchgear. There was a major setback for the business when one of its suppliers hit problems with its finances which, in turn, left the Wilsons facing difficulties of their own.

They recovered and went on to score in the export market selling to Brazil and Africa before landing their largest order - a £500,000 deal to supply large reactors to a Russian oilfield swiftly followed by the sale of their first large power transformer to Nigeria.

The design and manufacture of six power transformers bound for Nigeria strengthened the company's export division and helped to win an order for containerised switchgear packages to Iraq the following year.

In 2006 the company opened a tendering and design office in India – a precursor to WPDT, its Indian-based manufacturing division that is now part of the WPS group and employs more than 45 people in Chennai, India.

The following year saw the development of the first super low loss amorphous transformer, the product being introduced in 2007. WPS was the first power engineering company in the UK to be certified carbon neutral by The Carbon Neutral Company.

The Wilson e2, a super low loss amorphous transformer range, was launched at the Energy Event in Birmingham. Erika Wilson and marketing manager Lore Grohmann were occupied for hours rigging up a complex lighting array but it was worth the effort - the show was a success with Cranswick Gourmet Food becoming one of the early adopters of the new technology.

In 2009 retailer Tesco specified Wilson e2 transformers for all its new stores. The company gained a significant amount of industry recognition including speaker engagements for Erika at a number of sector specific events including a prestigious panel place at the National Energy Management Exhibition and CWIME exhibition, Berlin.

Above: *Westland Works in the late 1980s.* **Left:** *Members of the engineering team, test engineer, field engineer and transformer fitter.*

The same year saw a financial milestone with turnover exceeding the £10 million mark for the first time.

In 2011 the company became Wilson Power Solutions Ltd, creating a unified offering under one strong and modern brand. Launched in the same year was the Wilson e2, a super low loss amorphous transformer which received recognition from Business in the Community when WPS was highly commended in the Low Carbon Environment Leaders Awards.

Last year the Westland Works site, now in its 30th year, underwent a substantial refurbishment resulting in a modern open plan office with welcoming meeting rooms, improved on-site parking and new welfare facilities for both office and shop floor teams.

WPS very much remains a true family business. Earlier, when the business was incorporated it became known as RWD – Richard Wilson (Dencol) Ltd and both Dennis Wilson's son, Simon, and Colin Wilson's daughter, Erika, work in the business.

Above: *Westland Works site with 65kW solar PV installation.*
Top: *The Wilson Power Solutions team in 2015.*

Dennis, Colin and Simon Wilson also established an offshoot, Power and Distribution Transformers which became part of Wilson Power Solutions Ltd in 2011.

Joint managing director Simon Wilson said that the company, managed by the third generation of the Wilson family, is dedicated to helping customers find the best power distribution solution for their individual needs.

"We are passionate about what we do and are committed to giving advice with our customers' best interests at heart," he said.

Above: Members of the Marshall team, from left, Jack Marshall, Jamie Houston, Richard Cash, Ben Harris, Jarrod Thackray, Chris Marshall, Bryan Whitham, Karen Marshall and Tony Rawnsley.

J & L Marshall
Going it alone paid off

Joiners Jack Marshall and his uncle, Leonard Marshall, knew they were taking a gamble when they decided to go it alone.

They had the necessary skills to do their job well but running their own business was moving into unknown territory.

"We'd got a bit fed up working for other people so we decided to take the plunge," recalls Jack.

So in 1958 Leonard and Jack opened for business in a small workshop at the back of a row of terraced houses in Horsforth. Of course, success doesn't come overnight and the two men worked long and hard to establish their reputation for reliability and for producing quality work.

The business grew steadily and in 1970 Marshalls moved to new premises in Troy Hill, Horsforth, which gave them more room and improved facilities.

Leonard, who was Jack's guide and mentor, died several years ago but left a legacy of a business that was going places.

In 1975, Jack took another gamble and bought a site in New Road Side on the main Horsforth-Leeds Road consisting of a large wooden workshop and several lock-up garages. After handing over 'the biggest cheque of my life', Jack set about modernising the site.

The old wooden structure came down, replaced by a much larger workshop, offices were built, a builder's merchant depot was constructed, more land was developed for storage and premises fronting the main road were bought and converted into a hardware shop.

The firm took on skilled workers and added a general building section employing joiners, bricklayers and apprentices. Jack gradually found himself spending more time as an intermediary between local tradesmen and the large suppliers of bulk building materials. This was how the company established its niche in the local building industry.

In the 1990s the firm expanded its business by taking over and developing premises in Bradford Road, Otley, from where it provides building materials to the trade and to do-it-yourself enthusiasts. That part of the business was run by Robin Shuttleworth who would subsequently become a partner.

By the beginning of the new century Marshalls had become one of the area's best-known suppliers of building materials.

One of the firm's strengths is its ability to attract and retain highly-skilled workers.

This is amply illustrated by the firm's longest-serving employee, David Goodban, who joined Marshalls from school and has recently retired after completing 50 years' service. David is a skilled joiner but like many of the 20-strong workforce, can turn his hand to most jobs in the building trade. Most recently he ran the joiners' workshop.

The business has continued to expand and increased the size of its yard by purchasing half of the car sales yard next door and a former coach depot for additional storage space.

The current line-up also looks to have staying power! The yard and trade counter have been managed by Jamie Houston since 2001, and builder Tony Rawnsley has been with the firm for 25 years. The hardware store on site, selling goods and services from

carpet cleaners to key cutting, has been run by Bryan Whitham for more than 20 years.

Relative newcomers by Marshall's standards include yard and shop assistant Steve Pattinson who has been with the company for 10 years, shop assistant Richard Cash, yard assistants Chris Marshall and Jarrod Thackray, driver Keiran Thackray and Saturday worker Ben Harris.

The family suffered a devastating blow in August, 2013, when Jack's wife, Betty, and son, David, died. David had joined the company in 1972 and took on the running of the business. Betty had looked after the office work.

Marshalls is currently operated by a partnership of Jack Marshall, who is now in his 80s and still plays an active role in the company, and David's wife, Karen.

Marshalls remains the friendly, family-run business it has always been and will continue to supply building materials to the public and to the trade.

It prides itself on its excellent customer service and works hard to ensure its yard is fully stocked with only the best quality building materials.

"Only the best", has been good enough for Jack Marshall, his family and his workforce for more than half a century.

Below: *An aerial view of J & L Marshall, New Road Side, Horsforth*

Joseph Geldart & Sons
Highly respected funeral directors

The name of Joseph Geldart has been prominent in the Horsforth area of Leeds for more than 135 years and has become one of the most highly respected funeral directors in the area.

Joseph Geldart moved into the business after working as a joiner for several years. He started it from premises at Hopewell Terrace,

Top: The Joseph Geldart chapel of rest at New Road Side, Horsforth. *Right:* The property before work was started on the chapel of rest in 1969.

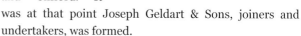

Horsforth, and was later joined by his two sons, Herbert and Clifford. It was at that point Joseph Geldart & Sons, joiners and undertakers, was formed.

"We are a five generation family business committed to giving the best possible care and service," said owner Mr Hadrian Cracknell.

The business grew steadily taking into consideration the fact that there were 11 funeral directors in Horsforth and 365 in the Leeds area at that time. When Joseph died he left the business to Herbert and Clifford but not long

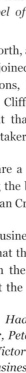

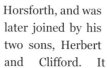

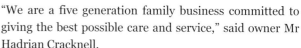

Left: Hadrian Cracknell (second from left) and his father, Peter (far right) with Harry Blackburn, (far left) and Victor Petty with the first Mercedes fleet bought by the business in the early 1980s.

afterwards Herbert passed away and Clifford carried the business on by himself.

In 1953 Clifford set on a young joiner called Peter Ambrose Cracknell. Peter worked alongside Clifford learning the trade of funeral directing. When Clifford died Peter bought the business. He was helped by his wife, Jean, who began to work with Peter in the firm.

As time went on the business was changing and chapels of rest were becoming more popular. Peter's skills as a joiner stood him in good stead when he built his first chapel of rest on Troy Hill at Horsforth. Later he constructed a purpose-built chapel at the premises at Hopewell Terrace.

Joseph Geldart & Sons continued to expand, both with joinery work and directing funerals. In the early 1980s a fleet of Mercedes cars was purchased and the firm also became carriage masters.

At the same time Peter's son, Hadrian, left school and joined the business after first serving his apprenticeship as a joiner.

Hadrian went to London to the highly respected firm of J.H. Kenyon which, at that time, were the royal funeral directors.

Hadrian had learned a lot of traditions such as paging - walking in front of the hearse wearing a top hat - and shouldering the coffin.

"This is instead of using wheels to take the coffin into the service. It looks more dignified and respectful," he said.

A decision was made to no longer carry on with the joinery side and focus on funerals. Horses had always been in the family's blood and in 1990 Peter and Hadrian came across an 1850s horse-drawn hearse that needed restoring.

Above: All horse-drawn carriages, which are fully restored and date back to 1850 and 1890, are pulled by a pair of black Friesians. They are led up by Norman Grayshon while Hadrian's stepdaughter, Paige, holds the reins.

Their joinery background once again proved useful. They got to work on completely restoring the hearse and it was finished a year after purchase.

After 70 years' absence, horse-drawn funerals were once again introduced to the streets of Leeds. Today Joseph Geldart & Sons is the only firm in Leeds to own and use working horses - not even Joshua Tetley's can say that!

"We have three carriages in total, with one Marston reproduction and two carriages dating back to 1850 and 1900," said Hadrian. "All our carriages are drawn by two black Friesian horses which are among the last of their breed in Leeds."

The firm's latest purchase is a 1958 Austin FX3 hearse used in the TV series "Heartbeat". This is currently undergoing restoration but is expected to be completed quite soon.

On leaving school recently, Paige, Hadrian's stepdaughter, joined the firm making it a five generation family business.

Hadrian also has a young son, Kaidan Peter Cracknell who, his father hopes, will in time become part of Joseph Geldart & Sons continuing the traditions of care set by generations before him.

"As an independent funeral director we believe we can offer the kind of care and service families expect from their funeral director," said Hadrian.

"We are sympathetic, we are family orientated and we organise a funeral to suit individual needs. Caring continues with the family long after the funeral is over."

Above: Geldart's has recently acquired a 1958 Austin FX3 hearse which has been featured in the TV series 'Heartbeat'.

Above: Hadrian Cracknell leads a funeral procession

Leeds & Yorkshire Housing Association
Providing affordable housing across Leeds, Scarborough, Whitby, Barnsley and Settle

Leeds & Yorkshire Housing Association Ltd was formed in 1979 through the merger of four associations, dating back individually as far as 1950.

Housing need had doubled between 1945 and 1950 because of war damage, the demolition of houses declared unfit for habitation and a booming population. Determined to do something about the housing shortage, Charles Charlesworth, a solicitor, set up the Leeds Tenants' Housing Society Ltd.

Yorkshire Cottage Housing Association Ltd was founded in 1952 with the aim of providing family housing and accommodation for the elderly. It helped retiring people to move from the cities to the coast or the country.

Aggrey Housing Ltd was formed in 1955 and was the country's first black and minority ethnic housing provider, describing itself as a trust providing homes to let for newcomers to Leeds. It was to house some of the thousands of overseas workers who came to Britain after the Second World War and promoted integration of BME people in Leeds.

Aire Valley Housing Ltd was founded in 1962 as a development consortium specialising in the design, construction and management of moderately priced homes for letting at a fair rent based on cost. Charlesworth's vision offered a new option for people in housing need – a middle ground between owning a home and being a private or local authority tenant.

The 1960s was a decade of rapid expansion and in 1961 the Housing Act made money available for housing associations to build new homes. Building projects were undertaken across the area and by the end of the decade, the collective assets of the societies were 837 homes worth £1.6m - 220 owned by the society.

During the 1970s, construction began on flats in St Ann's Square, Burley; Wood Lane, Headingley, and a sheltered scheme was created in Harehills. In 1971, the old Headingley Vicarage, which was to become the Leeds and Yorkshire Housing Association's head office in Shire Oak Road, was bought for £10,000.

Above: The Lomonds – one of the association's most recent developments designed to be in keeping with the style of other properties in the area, built to be energy efficient and thus affordable to run.

By the end of 1974, Leeds Tenants' Society had registered with the Housing Corporation, a non-departmental public body started in 1965 that funded new affordable housing and regulated housing associations in England.

In 1974, Charlesworth resigned as chairman of the Leeds Tenants' Society. By 1979 the four associations had amalgamated to form what is now Leeds and Yorkshire Housing Association.

During the 1980s the value of the association's assets doubled – from around £10m to £20m. Flats

Right: Chief Executive Lisa Pickard

Above: Spencer Place where the original meeting of Leeds Tenants' Housing Society took place in November, 1960. It is a property which was converted into self-contained flats for affordable rent, which is still owned by the association today. Right: The former Headingley Vicarage, Shire Oak road, now LYHA's Head Office.

were built at Belle Vue Road and at Brodrick Court, Headingley, and a new chair, Dr Don Halliday, was elected in 1988, taking over from S.R. Dalton, who had held the post since 1974.

The 1990s saw major improvement works to buildings which had been built in the 1960s and 1970s take place. Pitched roofs were added to flat-roofed buildings such as the blocks of flats at St Ann's Way, Headingley, and Towers Square in Meanwood. This resulted in improved appearance, increased energy efficiency and easier maintenance.

In Whitby, work began on the refurbishment of ten self-contained flats at West Cliff House.

In 1997, the association's secretary and son of the founder of Leeds Tenants' Society, Jack Charlesworth, retired and David Whitehead was appointed to the new position of chief executive. He described the association he was inheriting as "solid and financially sound with excellent potential".

Following the retirement of David Whitehead, Lisa Pickard was appointed as Chief Executive in 2012. Lisa joined LYHA from the Tenant Services Authority where she was assistant director, tenant standards. Lisa had worked in the sector for 18 years, holding a number of senior positions across several housing associations large and small and all based in the North of England.

Speaking about her new role new role at the time; Lisa said she felt very privileged to be a part of LYHA. "As we plan for the coming year, there are exciting and challenging times ahead which present opportunities to build on successes as well as grow and develop the organisation. I am very much looking forward to working with our customers, staff and stakeholders to help LYHA deliver its visions while at the same time, contributing to a wider agenda both regionally and nationally."

In the last four years, Lisa has transformed the Association ensuring it is fit for the future, able to respond to the challenges and risks whilst staying true to its original purpose. Lisa transformed LYHA from a surplus of £25k in 2012 to £1.2m in 2014 with a clear strategy to invest these surpluses to respond to the housing crisis and build much-needed new homes in Leeds and Yorkshire whilst ensuring they continue to invest in existing homes maintaining them to a high standard with a clear focus on improving affordability for its tenants.

Above: Former CEO David Whitehead who held the post for 14 years.

Leeds and Yorkshire Housing Association now owns and manages 1300 homes across Leeds and Yorkshire and has plans to provide more than 200 more much-needed new homes over the next three years.

The forward thinking, dynamic and progressive approach taken by the founding associations - tackling homelessness, promoting diversity, and developing affordable homes - is very much alive and embodied in Leeds & Yorkshire Housing Association's 21st Century mission to provide excellent quality homes and services that make a positive impact on people and communities.

Redmayne-Bentley
The friendly face of stockbroking

Stockbroker Redmayne-Bentley celebrates 140 years in business this year – a remarkable milestone for a company which represents the friendly face of stockbroking.

It was December 1875, when John Redmayne set up as a stockbroker at Leeds Stock Exchange under the name Redmayne & Co. From this small beginning, Redmayne-Bentley has firmly established itself as one of the UK's leading independently owned private client stockbrokers. As the firm has grown, it has not lost sight of its aim to make buying and selling shares more accessible.

Redmayne-Bentley's core values have stayed true to John Redmayne's mission, to open up the often shuttered world of stockbroking and make it accessible to everyone – a pledge echoed by managing partner David Loudon.

"Our values are central to all that we do and this commitment to our clients and staff has been acknowledged by industry experts. We work in an ever-evolving industry so it's paramount that everyone is up-to-date and compliant."

John Redmayne's early success was bound up with dealing in shares for private investors at the height of the great railway boom. His business thrived, even when the interest in railways declined, because of his overriding passion to provide a first class, highly efficient and, above all, friendly service to his clients.

Throughout the 20th century, talented and experienced new partners ensured that the firm's reputation flourished.

In 1923 Gavin Loudon, father of Redmayne-Bentley's current senior partner, Keith Loudon, joined the firm. After completing National Service, Keith joined in the late 1950s and became a partner in 1965.

A major landmark was reached that same year, when Gavin Loudon oversaw the merger of Redmayne and Co with F.W.

Above: *Celebrating the firm's 130th anniversary at London Stock Exchange. Senior partner Keith Loudon was invited to push the button to open the day's trading.*

Bentley and Co and J.W. Granger and Co, to form Redmayne-Bentley. The merged business moved to new premises at Albion Street giving it room to grow.

Redmayne-Bentley faced one of its most testing challenges in 1986 at the time of the so-called 'Big Bang' which led to far-reaching changes to stockbroking across the UK.

There were two schools of thought among the stockbroking fraternity over which direction to take – join forces with other regional firms to become large conglomerates focusing on advising wealthy clients or, offer a no-frills service to smaller clients.

Redmayne-Bentley decided to stay true to their values and remain independently owned. By providing a service accessible to all and continuing to offer a full range of services, Redmayne-Bentley stayed loyal to their growing list of private clients.

The firm's strong roots, its efficient and friendly service and expertise enabled it not just to survive, but to prosper and attract an increasing number of clients. The firm's reputation spread and as it did, stockbroking businesses across the country, attracted by the Redmayne-Bentley style of doing business, queued to join forces – and so a branch network was born.

Left: *Keith Loudon with Charlie Dimmock, star of the hit TV gardening show, 'Ground Force', and the face of a 'Share Aware' campaign in 1999.*

Left: The share shop at Redmayne-Bentley's headquarters on Bond Street, Leeds. **Above**: A busy day on the shop floor in the 1990s at the firm's former head office in Merrion Street, Leeds.

Redmayne-Bentley's achievements earned the firm a notable double award in 1998, when they were named Stockbroker of the Year and Best Regional Stockbroker at the Investors Chronicle Awards. More accolades were to follow over the next few years and the firm is especially proud of its recognition by the Investors in People scheme.

Despite being proud of its roots and traditions, the firm has never shied away from change and has always been at the cutting edge of new technology and fast-moving developments in the industry.

TV and radio facilities were installed, so the firm's staff could be called upon to provide informed comment on a variety of issues.

In 2001, Redmayne-Bentley brought its presence to the high street, with the opening of its stocks and shares shop in Leeds and over the following years opening of 13 new branches maintaining the firm's emphasis on providing an accessible service.

The business had a year to remember in 2005, when it celebrated its 130th anniversary - an event which saw senior partner, Keith Loudon, invited to London to push the button to open the day's trading at the London Stock Exchange. In 2012, more honours came in the shape of a Lifetime Achievement award for Keith at the City of London Wealth Management Awards.

The 2008 credit crunch saw volatile markets, but Redmayne-Bentley continued to grow with

Right: Leeds Stock Exchange in the 1960s. Keith Loudon is seated at the front, far left.

Left: A collection of artefacts tracing 130 years in business. This year another milestone was reached – the 140th anniversary.

the opening of its first overseas branch in Cork in 2009. In 2011 the head office in Leeds relocated to new premises at Bond Court which featured a new frontage, a conference room and private client meeting rooms.

The firm continues to expand its high street presence through acquisitions, which include the private client business Fyshe Horton Finney in 2013, and the recent opening of new branches in Tunbridge Wells and Market Harborough in 2015.

And so to the end of 2015 and another milestone beckons – 140 years in business. Founder John Redmayne would be justifiably proud of Redmayne-Bentley's success and even more so in the manner it has been achieved.

ACKNOWLEDGMENTS

The publisher would like to sincerely thank the following individuals and organisations for their help and contribution to this publication:

Mirrorpix

Wiki Commons - Brudenell School, Leeds courtesy of Lindosland – own work.

Wiki Commons